OFFICE FOR STANDARDS
IN EDUCATION

# *Guidance on the Inspection of* SPECIAL SCHOOLS

Issued by Her Majesty's Chief Inspector of Schools in England

London: HMSO

Office for Standards in Education
Alexandra House
29-33 Kingsway
London WC2B 6SE

BRUNEL UNIVERSITY
-- AUG 1997
LIBRARY

LC
3986
G7G84

© Crown copyright 1995
Applications for reproduction should be made to HMSO's Copyright Unit

ISBN 0 11 350068 8

# CONTENTS

# INTRODUCTION

This *Handbook* is published by Her Majesty's Chief Inspector of Schools (HMCI) for inspectors of special schools. It includes:

■ the *OFSTED Framework* for the inspection of schools under Section 9 of the Education (Schools) Act 1992; and

■ guidance on the conduct of inspections and on inspecting schools to the schedule for inspection in the *Framework*.

Part I consists of the **inspection requirements** which form part of the *Framework*. It sets out the principles on which inspections are based and the general requirements which are to be met by registered inspectors.

Part II provides **guidance on conducting inspections** in line with the inspection requirements. It focuses in particular on the role of registered inspectors leading inspections and outlines what they need to do before, during and after the inspection, *but it is important that all inspectors are aware of the contents*.

Part III includes the **inspection schedule** from the *Framework*, together with **guidance for inspectors on inspecting to the schedule**. The schedule sets out:

■ the specific requirements for evaluating and reporting on the work of the school and the standards achieved by pupils; and

■ the criteria which form the basis for arriving at judgements.

The guidance seeks to establish the main focus of inspection, provides advice on using the criteria and forming judgements in relation to each aspect of the schedule, and indicates key sources of evidence.

Guidance in the *Handbook* is intended to help ensure that the inspection process is of the highest quality and that judgements about a school are both fair and rigorous. A good inspection is one where:

■ judgements about the educational standards achieved by the school and the strengths and weaknesses in teaching and the other aspects inspected are objective, reliable and secure;

■ the main findings, and the key issues for action to raise educational standards achieved by pupils in the school, are clearly identified and reported to the school;

and, through the conduct of the inspection:

■ inspectors establish an effective working relationship with the school based on professionalism, sensitivity, and an understanding of the school's concerns and its circumstances;

■ the process is well planned and effectively managed;

■ there are good communications with the school which lead to a clear and shared understanding of what is involved at each stage;

■ inspectors readily explore issues with staff through professional dialogue;

■ judgements are made on the basis of the proper collection of the required evidence, through the application of appropriate criteria and the exercise of professional expertise; and

■ feedback to the school and the governing body, both orally and in writing, is clear and comprehensible.

Inspectors should leave the staff and governors feeling that they have gained from the contact with members of the team, as well as recognising the thoroughness of the evidence base and understanding and respecting the judgements which emerge. Those involved in running the school should feel that the inspection has provided a valuable component of their strategy for improvement.

# PART I

# THE OFSTED FRAMEWORK: INSPECTION REQUIREMENTS

## THE PURPOSE OF INSPECTION

**1** The purpose of inspection is to identify strengths and weaknesses so that schools may improve the quality of education they provide and raise the educational standards achieved by their pupils. The published report and summary report provide information for parents and the local community about the quality and standards of the school, consistent with the requirements of the *Parent's Charter*. The inspection process, feedback and reports give direction to the school's strategy for planning, review and improvement by providing rigorous external evaluation and identifying key issues for action. Inspection findings also provide a basis for the national evaluation of schools and the annual report of Her Majesty's Chief Inspector of Schools in England (HMCI).

## STATUTORY BASIS FOR INSPECTIONS BY REGISTERED INSPECTORS

**2** Inspection of a school[1] under Section 9 of the Education (Schools) Act 1992 (the 1992 Act) requires inspectors to report on:

> **the quality of the education provided by the school;**
>
> **the educational standards achieved in the school;**
>
> **whether the financial resources made available to the school are managed efficiently; and**
>
> **the spiritual, moral, social and cultural development of pupils at the school.**

**3** HMCI requires all registered inspectors to comply with the *OFSTED Framework* (the *Framework*) as a condition of registration, subject to any amendment issued by HMCI or to the contract specification for an individual inspection. Registered inspectors must be familiar with their statutory duties[2].

**4** The *Framework* forms the basis for assuring the standard of inspections. Judgements must be secured by appropriate evidence, and the consistent use of evaluation criteria, and informed by quantitative indicators. Guidance on the application of the *Framework* is provided in the *OFSTED Handbook* (the *Handbook*) which is issued in different versions to cater for the inspection of different types of school.

## INSPECTION OUTCOMES

**5** Inspection must lead to a full report, together with a summary of the report, which:

i   evaluates the school according to the *Framework*, any amendments required by HMCI, and the contract specification for the individual inspection;

---

1   Under the Education Act 1993 (the 1993 Act), pupil referral units (PRUs) are designated as schools. All references to schools include PRUs unless otherwise indicated.

2   The 1992 and 1993 Acts, and any subsequent legislation.

ii   identifies the strengths and weaknesses of the school; and

iii   gives the appropriate authority[3] for the school a clear agenda for the action required to improve it.

Inspection reports must follow the order prescribed in the *Framework*.

**6**   The *Framework* describes the obligations of registered inspectors in terms of both the **principles** portrayed in this section, and the **inspection schedule.** The latter sets out:

i   specific requirements for evaluating and reporting on the work of the school and the standards achieved by its pupils; and

ii   the criteria which form the basis for arriving at judgements. These are listed in the schedule under the heading: "Judgements should be based on the extent to which:".

## CODE OF CONDUCT FOR INSPECTORS

**7**   The right of entry to schools by inspectors brings with it important responsibilities. The code set out below outlines the principles which govern the conduct of inspections. Inspectors should uphold the highest professional standards in relation to all who are involved in the process before, during and after the inspection.

**Inspectors should:**

- carry out their work with professionalism, integrity and courtesy;

- evaluate the work of the school objectively;

- report honestly and fairly;

- communicate clearly and frankly;

- act in the best interests of the pupils at the school; and

- respect the confidentiality of personal information received during the inspection.

**8**   When inspecting schools, all registered inspectors must ensure that they and the members of their teams abide by this code of conduct.

---

3   The appropriate authority for a maintained school without a delegated budget is the Local Education Authority (LEA), and for an independent school the proprietor.  In all other cases it is the governing body.  References to the governing body in this Framework are to be taken in the case of independent schools as references to the proprietor or trustees. For all PRUs the LEA is the appropriate authority.

## THE STANDARD AND QUALITY OF INSPECTIONS

**9** Registered inspectors must ensure that their judgements are:

i **secure**, in that they are rooted in a substantial evidence base and informed by specified quantitative indicators;

ii **first-hand**, in that they are based largely on direct observation of pupils' and teachers' work;

iii **reliable**, in that they are based on consistent application of the evaluation criteria in the inspection schedule contained in this *Framework*;

iv **valid**, in that they accurately reflect what is actually achieved and provided by the school;

v **comprehensive**, in that they cover all aspects of the school set out in the inspection schedule and in the inspection contract specification; and

vi **corporate**, in that conclusions about the school as a whole reflect the collective view of the inspection team.

## THE INSPECTION PROCESS AND SCHOOL IMPROVEMENT

**10** The inspection process should help the school to raise educational standards. The governors and staff need to be involved as far as possible in the inspection. Where possible, inspectors should discuss with staff the context of work observed, its purpose, and the reasons why work is undertaken in a particular way. It is good practice for inspectors to test hypotheses with staff before judgements are finalised. In that an inspection, of necessity, takes place over a short period of time, inspectors should consider the school's own priorities for development, evidence about the past attainments of pupils and any evidence from the school's own analysis of its provision and standards.

## EQUAL OPPORTUNITIES

**11** Throughout the inspection, the requirements of the schedule should be applied in relation to **all** pupils in the school. Inspectors must ensure that the full range of age, gender, attainment, special educational need, ethnicity and background is taken into account, including the provision for, and attainment of, pupils for whom English is an additional language.

## TEAM COMPOSITION AND ASSIGNMENTS

**12** An inspection must be carried out by a registered inspector assisted by a team of trained inspectors which is sufficient and competent to conduct the inspection according to the requirements of the inspection schedule, unless modified by the contract specification, and Schedule 2 to the 1992 Act. The team must normally be capable of inspecting:

● those aspects of the school specified in the inspection schedule;

- as appropriate: National Curriculum subjects; the curriculum for pupils under five and students post-sixteen; vocational courses; and religious education in those schools which are required by statute to teach the subject according to an Agreed Syllabus[4]; and

- any other subject specified in the inspection contract.

The team must also include one or more inspectors charged with inspecting or co-ordinating the inspection of: equal opportunities issues; and, where relevant, the education of pupils for whom English is an additional language.

**13**  In the inspection of special schools, where teams are small, there must be a combination of phase and subject expertise but without undue fragmentation of the team. Inspection teams must be competent to inspect the full age range present in the school, including nursery provision. **Teams inspecting special schools must include expertise in the main types of special educational need represented in the school as well as the ability to ensure reasonable sampling of the subjects across the age range of pupils at the school.**

**14**  The registered inspector must include in the inspection team at least one member without personal experience in the management of any school or the provision of education in any school: the lay inspector[5]. No aspect of the inspection is to be barred to any inspector.

## QUALITY ASSURANCE REQUIREMENTS

**15**  To ensure that inspections are conducted to the highest standard, contractors for inspections are required to submit to OFSTED details of their quality assurance arrangements. These must cover:

- the induction, support, selection and deployment of inspectors;

- liaison with schools;

- the review and analysis of inspection evidence;

- ensuring that judgements about the school are corporate;

- ensuring the consistency, clarity and accuracy of reports and their compliance with requirements; and

- the use of feedback from the monitoring of inspections by OFSTED.

## TIME ALLOCATIONS FOR INSPECTIONS

**16**  In order to cover the work of the school adequately, **a specified minimum number of inspection days,** including those of the lay inspector, will be spent on direct inspection. The minimum tariff of days on site is set out in the relevant Instruction to Tenderers.

---

4   The 1992 Act as amended by Section 259 of the 1993 Act makes separate provision for the inspection of denominational religious education in those schools where it is provided; such inspections fall under Section 13 of the 1992 Act.

5   Paragraph 3(2) of Schedule 2 to the 1992 Act.

**17** Where the inspection contract specifies that there are extra features of the school to be inspected, inspection time beyond the minimum may also be specified. In all inspections, additional time is needed for:

- administration, and preparing for the inspection;
- analysis of documents;
- visiting the school and meeting the staff and governors;
- the pre-inspection meeting with parents;
- collating the findings of team members during and after the inspection;
- discussing findings with those responsible for the school; and
- writing the report and its summary.

## THE EVIDENCE BASE

**18** The registered inspector must compile, for each inspection, a *Record of Evidence* which contains the evidence collected by each member of the team. The detailed content of the *Record of Evidence* is prescribed in the *Handbook* and *Inspection Resource Pack*. The basic quantitative data about the school summarised in the *Headteacher's Form* are important evidence. The registered inspector is responsible for checking and where necessary correcting the data in the Form. OFSTED also provides data to enable inspectors to set the school's data in a national context.

## BEFORE THE INSPECTION

**19** The registered inspector must provide the appropriate authority and the headteacher[6] of the school with a list of the information and documents which are needed before the inspection, giving sufficient notice for the school to gather the items together and to complete the *Headteacher's Form* and *Statement*. The documents required are specified in Part II of the *Handbook*. In addition, the registered inspector will need to visit the school and prepare for inspection. The registered inspector should invite the appropriate authority to distribute the parents' questionnaire for return to the inspector before the meeting with parents.

**20** The appropriate authority for the school must arrange a meeting between the registered inspector and those parents of pupils at the school who wish to attend[7]. The registered inspector should ensure that parents' views are sought on aspects of the school specified in the *Handbook*. Parents' views contribute to the inspection evidence and must be taken into account in the course of the inspection. As the meeting takes place before the inspection, the registered inspector will not be able to comment on parents' views of the school. The registered inspector should discuss with the headteacher and the appropriate authority the key matters raised through the questionnaire and at the meeting. Where inspection reports refer to views expressed by parents, they should indicate the extent to which inspection findings support those views.

---

[6]   Or teacher in charge.

[7]   Schedule 2 to the 1992 Act.

## DURING THE INSPECTION

**21**   The sample of work inspected in a school must constitute an adequate cross-section. Wherever possible, the classes and work seen, and interviews with pupils, must be representative of all ages and levels of attainment. Work should be inspected in National Curriculum subjects as appropriate and in any other subjects or aspects specified in the inspection contract. Where a subject is not being taught at the time of the inspection, the report should state this fact clearly. In such a case, evaluation of pupils' attainment and progress in the subject should be based on the work previously completed by pupils, if this constitutes a sufficient sample, together with such other evidence as may be available. Members of the team should inspect the whole range of the school's work including extra-curricular activities. The inspection team should inspect acts of worship, except in schools where collective worship falls to be inspected under Section 13 of the 1992 Act[8] or where collective worship is not required.

**22**   The overall findings of the inspection should reflect the balance of evidence provided by the inspection team. The **Main Findings** and the **Key Issues for Action** must represent a corporate view.

**23**   Towards the end of the inspection it will be necessary for the registered inspector to ensure that all team members have indicated their evaluations clearly, and, with the team, to consider whether or not the school is failing, or likely to fail, to give its pupils an acceptable standard of education and thus requires special measures. The procedures to be adopted in such cases and the criteria on which to base a conclusion that a school falls into this category are set out in Annex 1 to this *Framework* and amplified in Part II of the *Handbook*.

## AFTER THE INSPECTION

**24**   The registered inspector must offer to discuss the findings of the inspection first with the headteacher, who may invite any staff of the school to be present. The appropriate authority must also be offered an oral report. This should occur as soon as possible after the inspection and before the inspection report is finalised. The registered inspector should present the findings of the report in such a way that they can be easily assimilated, for example, by using visual aids. The purpose of these discussions is not only to share with those concerned the outcomes of the inspection but to provide an opportunity for clarification of the Main Findings and Key Issues for Action.

**25**   It is also important to check on the factual accuracy of the inspection report. This is best done by offering the pre-publication text of the written report to the school after oral reports have been completed. Factual errors must be corrected. Only if such errors have a direct bearing on particular inspection judgements should the inspection team consider revising their judgements. Otherwise, there must be no modification of the judgements in the report.

---

8   See footnote 4 on page 11.

## THE INSPECTION REPORT AND SUMMARY

**26** The written report and a summary must be prepared by the registered inspector and sent to the appropriate authority for the school before the end of the period specified by HMCI in the inspection contract. Copies should also be sent to those specified in Section 209 of the 1993 Act or paragraph 9c of Schedule 2 to the 1992 Act. The report must be written in the order of the inspection schedule.

**27** The summary of the report should reproduce the Main Findings and Key Issues for Action sections of the inspection report together with a very brief contextual statement about the school indicating its type and size, a summary of the response to the parents' questionnaire, and the standard text specified in the *Handbook*.

**28** The inspection report and summary and those parts of the *Record of Evidence* required by HMCI must also be sent to OFSTED. Inspectors should retain their complete *Record of Evidence* for 12 months from the date of inspection. OFSTED may call on this record at any time during that period.

## MONITORING

**29** When an inspection is to be monitored by OFSTED to assess compliance of the registered inspector with the specified inspection procedures, the registered inspector will be notified and must afford HMI all necessary co-operation. HMI have access to all elements of the inspection.

Note: The Inspection Schedule from the *Framework* is integrated in Part III of this Handbook: 'The Inspection Schedule and Guidance on its use'.

# ANNEX 1

## SCHOOLS REQUIRING SPECIAL MEASURES

**1** Consideration of whether a school is failing, or likely to fail, to give its pupils an acceptable standard of education and therefore requires special measures should be based on the extent to which some or all of the following characteristics relating to the different sections of the Schedule are evident in the school.

### Educational standards achieved

◆ low attainment and poor progress in the subjects of the curriculum by the majority of pupils or consistently among particular groups of pupils. This will be evident in poor examination, National Curriculum assessment and other accredited results;

◆ regular disruptive behaviour, breakdown of discipline or high levels of exclusions;

◆ significant levels of racial tension or harassment;

◆ poor attendance by a substantial proportion of pupils or by particular groups of pupils, or high levels of truancy.

### Quality of education provided

◆ a high proportion of unsatisfactory teaching, including low expectations of pupils;

◆ failure to implement the National Curriculum;

◆ very poor provision for pupils' spiritual, moral, social and cultural development;

◆ pupils at physical or emotional risk from other pupils or adults in the school;

◆ abrasive and confrontational relationships between staff and pupils.

### The management and efficiency of the school

◆ ineffectiveness of the headteacher, senior management or governors;

◆ significant loss of confidence in the headteacher by the staff, parents or governors;

◆ demoralisation and disenchantment amongst staff or high levels of staff turnover or absence;

◆ poor management and inefficient use made of the resources, including finance, available to the school;

◆ poor value for money provided by the school.

2    A decision that a school requires special measures will depend on the combined weight of features. It is unlikely that one feature alone will result in such a decision, but where there is widespread and significantly poor attainment and progress, risk to pupils or the likelihood of a breakdown of discipline, the school will normally be judged to require special measures. In all such cases the headteacher and the governing body should be informed of the registered inspector's concern.

3    Where a judgement is made that the school is failing or likely to fail to give its pupils an acceptable standard of education, the registered inspector has a duty to inform HMCI and express the opinion in the report stating whether or not HMCI agrees. Further guidance on the procedures to be followed are included in Part II of the *Handbook*.

# Part II

# GUIDANCE ON INSPECTION REQUIREMENTS: THE CONDUCT OF INSPECTIONS

This part of the *Handbook* provides guidance on the management and conduct of inspections in line with the inspection requirements set out in the *Framework*. It is structured to reflect the sequence of work before, during and after the time the inspection team spends in the school.

Responsibility for the conduct and management of the inspection, and for the inspection report, rests with the registered inspector named in the contract. While this guidance focuses on the role of the registered inspector, it is important that all team members are aware of the inspection requirements and comply with them, particularly the Code of Conduct.

## CODE OF CONDUCT FOR INSPECTORS

**1**    The *Framework* includes a Code of Conduct which is a set of principles and must govern the conduct of inspections. The principles should be followed by all inspectors throughout the inspection process, and underpin the high standards of conduct which are expected of those involved in the inspection of a school. Breach of the code is a serious matter, and could in extreme cases result in the loss of registration. Amplification of the Code of Conduct follows.

**Inspectors should carry out their work with professionalism, integrity and courtesy.**

**2**    All inspectors need to recognise that the process of inspection is demanding for schools, and that it can be very stressful. The way in which the inspection is conducted should contribute to reducing any stress to a minimum. The conduct of inspectors should instill confidence, minimise disruption and anxiety and ensure the co-operation of staff and members of the appropriate authority. Inspectors should be well-briefed and treat all those involved with the school with respect.

**3**    Inspectors must carry out their statutory duties and maintain their independence and objectivity, and that of OFSTED. The term 'registered inspector' must be used only in connection with inspections undertaken for OFSTED. Inspectors must not use their position as inspectors to secure further employment where it may reflect on their impartiality or compromise the integrity of the inspection. In contributing to educational debate or working in other professional capacities, inspectors must not undermine their capacity to conduct inspections for OFSTED.

**Inspectors should evaluate the work of the school objectively.**

**4**    The inspection has to be undertaken without bias or preconceptions about the school. No inspector should take part in an inspection if they have a close previous relationship with the school. Inspectors must be absolutely impartial, and be seen to be impartial, in their treatment of all those with whom they come into contact. Judgements must be based on sound evidence which has been carefully weighed, collected from a range of sources and firmly based on the criteria in the inspection schedule. Inspectors must be particularly careful to avoid making premature judgements.

**Inspectors should report honestly and fairly.**

**5**  Inspectors must report on their findings without fear or favour. They must report on positive features and strengths but must not refrain from identifying and reporting on difficult issues which will need resolution for the school to improve. When inspectors come to their conclusions, issues need to be considered carefully and minor issues should not be given undue prominence. The resulting report should be as fair and just a representation of the school as possible, with all recommendations firmly supported by evidence. The oral reports of inspection findings to staff and members of the appropriate authority must be consistent with the final report.

**Inspectors should communicate clearly and frankly.**

**6**  Inspectors must maintain an open dialogue with all those involved in the school without compromising the confidentiality of information about individuals. Parents, teachers and other staff, pupils and members of the appropriate authority need to understand fully the purposes of inspection, the role they play in the process and what is required of them.

**7**  Good communication is particularly important during the oral reports to staff and the appropriate authority. Complex information and possibly unwelcome judgements should be conveyed as simply and accessibly as possible.

**Inspectors should act in the best interests of pupils at the school.**

**8**  Inspectors enter schools in a position of authority, and the safety and well-being of the pupils must be a prime concern. Nothing an inspector does should cause a child distress or anxiety. Inspectors should ensure that no situation arises which could be construed as calling into question the propriety of the relationship between inspector and pupil, for example, talking to individual pupils in isolation or singling out individual pupils for undue attention.

**9**  If inspectors observe or hear of anything which causes them concern about the safety or well-being of the pupils then the registered inspector must report these concerns to the headteacher or appropriate authority. If, in the interests of the safety and well-being of the pupils, the registered inspector deems it inappropriate to do so, then he or she must inform the appropriate external agency, for example, where relevant, the Social Services Department. If indiscipline or bad behaviour of pupils is observed when a teacher is present, an inspector should not interfere unless the safety or welfare of pupils is endangered.

**Inspectors should respect the confidentiality of personal information received during the inspection.**

**10**  Inspectors will be privy to information about individuals during the inspection. Such information is confidential. The identification of individuals for criticism should not form any part of the formal inspection report or of the discussion with the appropriate authority and this confidentiality must be respected after the inspection. During the course of their work inspectors should not seek access to confidential staff appraisal information; this is not part of the inspection.

**11**  The findings of the inspection are confidential to the team and the school until the final report is published.

## THE EVIDENCE BASE

**12** Systematic collection and evaluation of evidence is at the heart of inspection. A key part of the registered inspector's role is to manage the evidence base and ensure that sound and fair judgements derive from it. The nature of the *Record of Evidence* of inspection which registered inspectors will assemble before and during the inspection is outlined below. Further guidance on this is included in the *Inspection Resource Pack* for inspectors.

### The Record of Evidence

**13** The registered inspectors must compile for each inspection a *Record of Evidence* (*RoE*) which summarises all the relevant evidence collected by the inspection team. The *RoE* should:

   i    provide a format for recording the key inspection evidence in a form which assists writing the report;

   ii   secure the evidence on which judgements in the report are based in case of legal challenge;

   iii  enable HMCI to have access to a formal *RoE* as part of OFSTED's quality assurance procedures.

**14** OFSTED will retrieve from inspection reports and use parts of the *RoE* to provide a national evidence base to inform HMCI's Annual Report[9] and other reports on aspects of the education system.

**15** The *Record of Evidence* consists of:

### Data from OFSTED

This may include a Pre-inspection Context and School Indicator (PICSI) report containing: key performance data about the school from earlier years to enable trends to be identified; information about the social and economic characteristics of the area in which the school is situated; and comparative data, although for many special schools it is not appropriate to report their standards in comparison with national standards.

### The Headteacher's Form and Statement[10]

A minimum core of quantitative data about the school, provided in standard format, together with the headteacher's commentary on the school which should include a brief description of the characteristics of the school, its pupils, and those features of the area it serves which influence its work.

---

9    As required by the 1992 Act.

10   References to headteacher include the teacher in charge of a pupil referral unit (PRU).

### The Observation Form

A basis for recording evidence and judgements from observation of lessons and other inspection activities, including scrutiny of pupils' work, discussion with pupils and analysis of assessment and examination data.

### The Subject Profile

A summary which draws together the evidence for each of the core subjects; and a set of grades which reflects judgements in these subjects.

### The School Profile

A summary which draws together the evidence compiled by the team of inspectors during the inspection; and a set of grades to reflect the corporate judgements of the inspection team.

### Any Other Evidence

Any other working notes that the registered inspector wishes to retain within the *RoE*.

## BEFORE THE INSPECTION

## INITIAL CONTACT WITH THE SCHOOL

**16** First contacts, written and spoken, between the registered inspector and the school are particularly important in establishing a good working relationship and setting the tone and style for the whole inspection process. They also provide a first insight into the nature of the school.

**17** The registered inspector should contact the appropriate authority[11], usually via the headteacher, to agree dates for the beginning and end of the inspection. These should be confirmed in writing. Any difficulties should be resolved by negotiation, but in the unlikely event that agreement cannot be reached, OFSTED should be informed. OFSTED will then seek views and fix the date.

**18** The registered inspector should subsequently contact the headteacher to:

i    arrange an initial visit to the school , discuss its purpose and negotiate a programme;

ii   offer to meet the teaching and non-teaching staff during the initial visit to explain the inspection process and the aspects of the school's work to be covered;

iii  offer a meeting to discuss the inspection process with representatives of the appropriate authority. Normally this will occur during the initial visit; and

iv   discuss the information which will be required from the school before the inspection, explaining why it is needed, and make arrangements for its collection.

---

11  The appropriate authority is usually the governing body of the school, but in schools without a fully delegated budget and in PRUs it is the LEA.

The following should be requested as appropriate:

- a completed *Headteacher's Form* and *Statement*;

- school prospectus;

- school development plan or equivalent planning document;

- copy of last annual report to parents (not required for PRUs);

- minutes of meetings of the appropriate authority for the last 12 months;

- staff handbook (if available);

- curriculum plans, policies and guidelines or schemes of work, already in existence;

- other policy documents which are available in the school;

- a programme or timetable of the work of the school for the period of the inspection (deadline to be negotiated); and

- other information the school wishes to be considered, including any documents about, and the outcomes of, any school self-evaluation activities.

If the inspection is to take place early in the school year, the registered inspector should advise the school that pupils' work from the previous year will be needed.

**19** The registered inspector should send the *Headteacher's Form* and *Statement* to the school for completion before the initial visit. Where a PICSI report is provided by OFSTED, this should also be sent to the school for discussion during the initial visit.

**20** It is important that schools do not feel that substantial documentation must be produced specially for the inspection. Some additional items, for example, attendance registers, samples of pupils' records and reports to parents, may be required by inspectors during the week of the inspection, often to be used in conjunction with the samples of pupils' work. **On no account should inspectors issue additional forms to the school for completion, beyond those prescribed by OFSTED.**

## INITIAL VISIT

**21** The initial visit to the school should be carefully planned through discussion with the head and arranged at a mutually convenient time. The timing of the visit requires considerate negotiation as the meeting will draw heavily on the headteacher's time.

**22** The registered inspector should explain to the school that analysis of the school's documentation and other information collected during the initial visit is used to give other members of the team a background to the inspection and to help the registered inspector to identify any particular issues on which the inspection might focus. The registered inspector should invite the headteacher and appropriate authority to identify particular aspects that they would like inspectors to focus on, provided this can be done within the scope of the *Framework* and the contract.

**23**   During the initial visit, the registered inspector should :

i   discuss with the headteacher: the inspection process, including lesson or session observation procedures; other aspects of methodology including the appropriateness of making judgements of attainment against national averages; and post-inspection events;

ii   confirm the composition of the inspection team, provide information about how the team will be deployed and discuss coverage of curriculum and other aspects of the school's work. The contract provides for the registered inspector to supply the school with a brief summary of the background of the team members. If for any reason it is not possible to detail the team deployment at the time of the initial visit this should be done as soon as possible after the visit. In any case it must be done in accordance with the timetable set out in the contract;

iii   resolve any difficulties the headteacher may have found in completing the *Headteacher's Form* and *Statement*;

iv   if a PICSI report has been provided, check it with the headteacher for any inconsistencies and begin to form a description of the characteristics of the school (section 3.1 of the report) for agreement with the headteacher and appropriate authority;

v   collect the documentation requested;

vi   agree the additional information to be made available during the inspection, for example:

◆ samples of pupils' work;

◆ pupils' records and reports;

◆ statements and reviews;

◆ teachers' planning and assessment documents including guidelines or schemes of work if not provided earlier;

◆ registers of attendance; and

◆ any other information the school feels would be helpful to the inspection;

vii   gather pre-inspection evidence for the *School Profile* through discussion with the headteacher, other staff and representatives of the appropriate authority if available;

viii   arrange for whole school and class timetables of teaching programmes to be made available. Inspectors should make it clear to schools for which the National Curriculum applies, that they expect to see teaching in the core subjects and whatever else the school does as part of its normal programme for the period of the inspection. They should not require the school to adjust its curriculum;

ix   identify when - in reception classes - the school begins to teach to the programmes of study of the National Curriculum;[12]

x   give a clear indication of the kind of discussions likely to be required with individual members of staff, keeping demands on their time to a minimum, especially where they carry multiple responsibilities. Where it is possible to agree a programme of discussions with key staff in advance of the inspection, this should be done;

---

[12]   Legally, pupils should start the National Curriculum no later than their fifth birthday.

xi   discuss arrangements for looking at all the work available for a sample of pupils including any particular arrangements needed, where, for example, the inspection is at the start of a new year;

xii   meet the staff to explain how the inspection will be conducted and how feedback will be given to teachers.

**24**   At or before the initial visit, the registered inspector needs to negotiate with the headteacher the date and time for the pre-inspection meeting with parents to seek their views of the school. It is important to note that:

- the appropriate authority is responsible for arranging the meeting;

- the meeting should be held before the inspection;

- parents should be given three weeks' notice of the meeting; and

- all parents of pupils registered at the school at the time of the inspection should be invited.

A sample letter, including a suggested agenda for the meeting, to be used by the appropriate authority for inviting parents to the meeting, is included in the *Inspection Resource Pack*.

**25**   A standard questionnaire for parents is included in the *Inspection Resource Pack* and inspectors should encourage schools to use this. If the school agrees to issue the questionnaire, arrangements should be made for its return, in confidence, to the registered inspector. The questionnaire should be issued to the parents of all pupils on the roll of the school. The registered inspector should make it clear to the school that a summary of the parents' responses will be included in the inspection report.

**26**   The consensus of views expressed by parents in the meeting and through the questionnaires should be shared with the school and the appropriate authority.

**27**   The registered inspector should also, at the initial visit, discuss with the headteacher the practicalities of giving oral reports of the inspection findings. Oral reports must be offered to the headteacher, who may invite other staff to be present, and subsequently to the appropriate authority. Mutually convenient dates will need to be arranged for these meetings. Inspectors should explore with the headteacher the appropriateness and practicality of sharing inspection findings with staff holding positions of responsibility.

**28**   During the initial visit it is particularly useful if the registered inspector can be shown around the school to meet staff and children, become familiar with the site(s) and gain first impressions of the school to provide the team with a background to their visit.

**29**   The registered inspector should discuss courtesies and domestic arrangements, for example the introduction of team members on arrival at the school, access to the building outside normal school hours and a base for the team. Schools are under no obligation to provide a meeting room for inspectors, but should do so if they can. In some schools there may not be a convenient space for the team, in which case the registered inspector should arrange to use suitable accommodation nearby.

## PREPARING THE TEAM FOR INSPECTION

**30**   The registered inspector is responsible for ensuring that members of the team are thoroughly prepared for the inspection and that their work is well planned. It is important that teams establish a corporate approach and style which are maintained with consistency.

### Deployment of the team

**31**   Within the scope of the contract the registered inspector should plan and agree with the team members a realistic allocation of responsibilities to ensure that:

i   all aspects in the Schedule and subjects, particularly the core subjects, and areas of learning are inspected;

ii   assignments of all team inspectors, including the lay inspector, take account of any special interests and expertise;

iii   the lay inspector is given assignments across a range of aspects of the school's work to allow a full contribution to be made to the inspection and to the corporate judgements; except in a one-teacher school, the lay inspector should not spend less than a full day in the school;

iv   the team is informed about any pre-inspection and post-inspection team meetings and deadlines for writing.

### Pre-inspection analysis

**32**   The pre-inspection sections of the *School Profile* must be completed to provide a brief commentary for the team and to identify inspection issues specific to the school. This should take account of any significant points from the initial visit or raised at the parents' meeting, the outcomes of any self evaluation measures, issues for inspection identified by the school, and analyses of the PICSI report (where issued) and other information.

### Briefing the team

**33**   Through a meeting with team members, or by other means, the registered inspector should:

i   ensure that the team is thoroughly briefed about the school and the inspection, and receives all pre-inspection comments and analyses;

ii   distribute copies of school documentation relating to the areas of responsibility of team members;

iii   using class timetables, draw up a programme for inspection which includes inspection of all year groups and, as far as possible, the full range of subjects, courses or areas of learning and the work of all teachers, as well as the other evidence needed to cover the requirements of the schedule;

iv   ensure that team members understand the arrangements made for the scrutiny of pupils' work and analysis of teachers' planning;

v   prepare timetables and agendas for team meetings including the arrangements for securing corporate judgements; and

vi   establish clear procedures to ensure adherence to the Code of Conduct for inspection.

## THE PARENTS' MEETING

**34**    The parents' meeting is an opportunity to inform parents about the inspection and to fulfil the statutory requirement to seek parents' views on the school. The registered inspector should be accompanied by a member of the inspection team to record the views of parents. The meeting can only be attended by parents of pupils registered at the school at the time of the inspection. Members of the staff and the appropriate authority may attend only if they have a child currently attending the school. The headteacher or chair of the appropriate authority may, of course, wish to be present at the start of the meeting to introduce the registered inspector.

**35**    The registered inspector should:

     i     explain the purpose of the meeting and provide an agenda;

     ii    explain and answer questions on the nature of the inspection and the report;

     iii   seek parents' views about the school and its context; and

     iv   note, but make no comment on the validity of those views.

**36**    The registered inspector should make clear at the start of the meeting that parents' views will be taken into account as part of the inspection. Parents should be asked to couch their comments in general terms as far as possible, so as to avoid naming individuals.

**37**    The registered inspector should seek parents' views on:

     i     pupils' attainment and progress;

     ii    the attitudes and values which the school promotes;

     iii   the information which the school provides for parents, including reports;

     iv   the help and guidance available to pupils;

     v     homework and the contribution it makes to pupils' progress;

     vi   pupils' behaviour and attendance;

     vii   the part parents play in the life of the school; and

     viii   the school's response to their suggestions and complaints.

## DURING THE INSPECTION

### The role of the registered inspector

**38**   The registered inspector is the manager of the inspection team and the whole inspection process, and is the first point of reference for everyone involved in the inspection. Effective management and organisation of the team on a day-to-day basis are crucial to the success of the inspection. It is the registered inspector's responsibility to ensure that judgements are secure, first-hand, reliable, valid, comprehensive and corporate. The registered inspector is also responsible for producing the inspection report and the summary of the report. These must be clear and helpful to the appropriate authority and parents.

**39**   The registered inspector should:

i   ensure that inspectors are consistent in their approaches to the collection and recording of evidence;

ii   be prepared to adjust the workload of individual inspectors as circumstances dictate;

iii   monitor and, if necessary, intervene in the work of the team so as to ensure compliance with the *Framework*;

iv   undertake direct inspection such as observing work in classrooms, sampling pupils' written work, and holding discussions with staff and pupils; and

v   provide systems for the collection, collation and validation of evidence within the team; review and analyse this evidence, keeping the *Record of Evidence* up to date.

**40**   The registered inspector should meet the headteacher regularly to agree administrative details, obtain further information, clarify inspection issues and resolve any difficulties which might emerge during the inspection.

### Team inspectors' assignments

**41**   Inspectors need to plan and use their time carefully and efficiently to achieve the coverage required. They should be sensitive to the impact of the inspection on teaching and support staff. Inspection of some aspects of the school's work will require contributions from the whole team, and will need to be co-ordinated by one of the inspectors. Such aspects include, for example, the assessment of:

i   the standard of reading of individual pupils; other aspects of English capability such as speaking, listening and writing; and numeracy;

ii   equality of opportunity for different groups of pupils; and

iii   pupils' spiritual, moral, social and cultural development.

### Gathering the inspection evidence

**42**   Within their assignments individual inspectors should allocate time to collect the range of core evidence on which the judgements of the team must be based. This includes:

i     the inspection of teaching and of pupils at work in classrooms and other areas;

ii    discussion with pupils, for example, to assess their understanding and knowledge of different subjects and their attitudes to work and their life at school;

iii   hearing pupils read, where appropriate;

iv    the scrutiny of a representative sample of pupils' work;

v     discussions with staff, especially those with management responsibilities;

vi    the scrutiny of teachers' plans, records of National Curriculum tests and teachers' assessments, details of any assessment undertaken on entry to nursery or reception classes and other measures or indicators of attainment and progress used by the school;

vii   the scrutiny of a sample of statements of special educational need, annual reviews and individual education plans;

viii  with the agreement of the appropriate authority and where practicable, visits to a small sample of schools where re-integration of pupils takes place.

The evidence should be recorded on *Observation Forms* as the inspection proceeds. A complete specification of evidence is given earlier in this Part of the *Handbook* (paragraphs 12-15).

## Review of documentary evidence

**43**  Documentary evidence provided by the school must be assimilated and fully considered. Analysis of material prior to inspection forms the basis of pre-inspection commentaries relating to aspects of the *Framework*. Other documentary evidence is needed during inspection, for example for pupils' records and reports. Time should be set aside during the inspection for the consideration of this material.

**44**  Statements of aims, policies and documents relating to procedures should be evaluated in terms of their impact on the work of the school. Inspectors should determine whether intentions are followed through into effective practice.

## Observation of lessons and other activities

**45**  While the school is in session the inspection team should aim to spend at least 60% of its time observing lessons, sampling pupils' work and talking to pupils.

**46**  Where possible, all classes and teachers should be visited when teaching, whatever the size of the school. The load on teachers should be spread as evenly as possible. Inspectors should visit classes taught by replacement or supply teachers and by students in training: in these cases the criteria applied for evaluation are the same as for other classes. Time must be given to sample a representative selection of all the work of the school to ensure the validity of the inspection findings. This should include:

◆  observation of a balanced range of lessons with pupils of all ages, capabilities and disability in all areas of learning and subjects of the curriculum of the school;

◆  where justifiable and practicable, observation of pupils in other settings such as local mainstream schools and colleges, work experience placements and independent life skills programmes;

◆ examination of previous work, records, annual reviews and other evidence of achievement to assess overall progress and the coverage of learning experiences, over a period of time;

◆ observation of pupils taught individually;

◆ observation of pupils receiving therapy inputs which give them greater access to a broadly based and balanced curriculum. This does not include psychotherapy or any other therapy which is of a confidential nature;

◆ observation of pupils in residential settings and undertaking extra-curricular activities.

**47**  In all schools, particularly small ones, registered inspectors should ensure a balance between achieving adequate coverage of the schedule and allowing teachers respite from continuous inspection for a reasonable period each day.

**48**  Lessons or sessions observed should be from the normal programme of work: inspectors should not impose or require changes to that programme. Schools should, however, ensure that work in the core subjects of English, mathematics and science is in evidence during the inspection.

**49**  The time spent in observing lessons or sessions is likely to vary in duration, but should be long enough to gather sufficient evidence for work to be evaluated.

**50**  Effective inspection involves joining individual pupils and groups to look at their work and to discuss it with them. It also includes careful observation of teaching, including the organisation of work for pupils as a class, in groups or individually. Both need to be done so as not to disrupt either teaching or learning and note-taking should be as unobtrusive as possible.

**51**  In some classrooms a variety of activities including outdoor play may be taking place at the same time. Sometimes inspectors will need to concentrate on one subject or area of learning. At other times they should spend sufficient time with the class to gather evidence about all that is taking place: the evidence can then be passed on to team members having responsibility for particular subjects, areas of learning, or aspects of work. **Every effort should be made to avoid classes being visited by a procession of inspectors, each seeking evidence solely in their area of interest.**

**52**  There should not normally be more than one inspector in a class at any time unless the class teacher agrees and there is a particular reason for so doing.

**53**  Inspection must include assemblies, and extra-curricular activities, including sports, if they are offered, and may encompass educational visits where justifiable and practicable.

### Talking with pupils

**54**  A key source of evidence of the attainment and attitudes of pupils of all ages is discussion with them at work and play. This should be structured so as to explore their knowledge and understanding of current and recent work, and their ability to apply knowledge in different contexts. In addition to providing evidence of what has been learned, skilful discussion can give an indication of how well pupils understand what has been taught and whether the teaching and the tasks set for them are too hard, too easy or about right. Some discussion may take place with groups of children outside the classroom. In all classroom observations, it is important to listen to:

- pupils' incidental talk and comments;

- their contribution in class;

- their responses to questions;

- the questions initiated by them; and

- their views, feelings and comments expressed in discussions.

**Sampling pupils' work**

**55**   Pupils' previous and current work provide an essential source of evidence of both attainment and progress, as well as an insight into the curriculum and teaching. In addition to the work routinely seen during the observation of lessons, inspectors will need to look at the samples of work agreed between the registered inspector and the headteacher during the initial visit.

**56**   It is helpful if the sampling takes place near the beginning of the week in order to follow up the issues raised. Judgements on the sample should be made in relation to other work observed during the inspection.

**57**   The sample should include:

   i    the work of as large a sample of pupils as possible, relating observations to their statements of special educational need, annual reviews, and individual education plans;

   ii   portfolios of assessed work where available.

**58**   For each pupil, examples of past and present work should be available in order to establish the range of work covered over time and to evaluate evidence of progress. Inspectors find it helpful to have pupils' records available alongside their written work, including individual education plans, annual reviews or statements of special educational need. It is also helpful to follow up the scrutiny of this work through discussion with the pupils. It is helpful if salient points in the pupils' educational history and statements are provided alongside the samples of work.

**59**   Judgements about the progress and achievement of pupils must be informed by close observation of what they know, understand and can do in relation to their capabilities and previous attainment. For pupils whose steps in learning are small, which may not be readily identifiable in a particular lesson, every endeavour should be made to evaluate the quality of their responses to a planned environment. These evaluations should be complemented by other sources of evidence which describe progress and attainment over a period of time.

**60**   For pupils with conditions that are degenerative, judgements should be made about the overall quality of the environment provided and the quality of those planned experiences relevant to the pupils' needs.

**61**   Registered inspectors will also need to ensure that during the week of the inspection a sufficient sample of literary and numeracy skills is taken by:

i   hearing at least three pupils from each year group read, and more in Years 2 and 3. Where there is cause for concern about reporting standards in a particular class, or more generally, more children should be heard to read to help determine the extent and causes of poor standards of reading. Pupils should read from published materials or schemes, library books, and samples of their own writing. In some small schools there may not be many children in a year group, but where possible at least three pupils in each year group should be heard to read;

ii   through discussion and questioning, assessing pupils' attainment in numeracy, particularly at the end of key stages.

### Discussion with staff, the appropriate authority and others involved in the work of the school

62   Headteachers and registered inspectors alike value a daily meeting to agree administrative details, discuss any matters of concern, clarify inspection issues and obtain further information. These contribute a great deal to the smooth running of an inspection and the maintenance of good relationships.

63   Discussions with the headteacher, representatives of the appropriate authority, staff with particular management responsibilities, class teachers, support agencies and care staff provide important sources of evidence relating to roles and responsibilities, procedures and policies. They are also essential to the professional dialogue between staff and inspectors which contributes positively to the inspection of schools and helps inspectors to establish the context of what is seen. Discussion with teachers, especially at the end of lessons or sessions, is always desirable, but it may not always be possible to have more than a brief exchange. However, the work of teachers should be acknowledged and as many opportunities as possible found for professional dialogue. Such dialogue might involve clarification about the context of the lesson or session and of future work, as well as providing brief evaluation of the quality of work seen in the lesson, where that is possible. Inspectors should not, however, allow discussion about the work and its evaluation to stray into giving on-the-spot advice, nor adopt an advisory role in any part of the inspection.

64   Meetings with staff and representatives of the appropriate authority should take place at mutually convenient times. A list of points to provide a focus for discussion should be indicated in advance to give those concerned time to think about the issues. Care should be taken that meetings do not make unreasonable demands on teachers' time, for instance their break times.

Where a teacher has more than one school-wide responsibility, it is an efficient use of time to arrange for one inspector to cover a sample of the most important issues related to that teacher's responsibilities at a single meeting, rather than resort to a succession of interviews.

65   Discussions with non-teaching staff, including nursery nurses, classroom assistants, secretaries, voluntary helpers and any visiting specialists, eg. speech therapists, also provide valuable information and contribute to involving all staff in the inspection.

## ORAL REPORTING TO CO-ORDINATORS AND OTHER TEACHERS WITH SIGNIFICANT RESPONSIBILITIES

**66**   Towards the end of the inspection, oral reports on the inspection findings in particular subjects or aspects of the schools' work should be offered where appropriate to those with significant responsibilities. The school may wish other staff, such as the headteacher or deputy, to be present. However, in small schools where staff carry multiple subject/aspect responsibilities it may not be possible to give feedback to co-ordinators individually. In this case, feedback may take place to the headteacher or to the staff as a whole as part of more formal reporting of inspection findings. The extent of other oral reports should be agreed by the registered inspector and the head. It is important that the format and arrangements for oral reporting are consistent and are fully understood. Where possible, they should be negotiated with the school before the inspection. A clear understanding should be reached as to who will receive feedback. Specific issues relating to a particular lesson or observed practice which could be identified with a teacher must not be raised with senior staff unless the issue has also been raised with the particular teacher concerned.

## DATA MANAGEMENT

**67**   During the inspection the registered inspector will need to manage and analyse the data gathered by the team in order to:

i   monitor and ensure appropriate coverage of subjects, courses, year groups, key stages, and pupils' individual needs; and

ii   provide a picture of the emerging evidence to inform team discussion and the making of corporate judgements.

## HEALTH AND SAFETY

**68**   It is unlikely that the registered inspector is an expert in health and safety matters. Inspectors are not therefore required to carry out an audit of health and safety practice. The registered inspector must, however, record and report on those aspects of the school, which, in his or her opinion, constitute a threat to health and safety.

**69**   In order to meet these requirements the registered inspector should:

i   check that the school is aware of the need to comply with statutory requirements for health and safety[13] and has clear procedures to identify and control health and safety risks;

ii   comment on any health and safety risks observed during inspection;

iii   record any health and safety irregularities and bring these to the attention of the headteacher and the employer;[14] and

---

[13]  Detailed commentary on the statutory requirements for health and safety in schools and on how schools should manage these aspects can be found in the HSE publication *Managing Health and Safety*, ISBN 0-71-760770-4.

iv   alert the Health and Safety Executive where there is an imminent risk of serious injury and the employer appears likely to refuse to remedy the situation.

**70**   The registered inspector must not only ascertain that the school has a health and safety policy and is aware of statutory requirements but should also judge whether the school has a responsible attitude towards the education and training of pupils in safe practice. Further guidance is given in Section 5.3 of Part III of the *Handbook*.

## TEAM MEETINGS

**71**   The main purpose of team meetings is to arrive at an accurate and thoroughly tested corporate view of pupils' attainments and progress, and the factors which contribute to or detract from these outcomes, i.e. the quality of education provided, provision for pupils' spiritual, moral, social and cultural development, how well the school is led and whether its resources are managed efficiently.

**72**   Well-structured and managed meetings help a team to give proper consideration to the evidence, to address the judgements required by the *Framework* and to spend discussion time on issues which are particularly important.

**73**   Registered inspectors should establish at these meetings a sense of common purpose based on good working relationships, and a clear understanding of respective responsibilities within the team.

**74**   Where the size of team and duration of inspection allow, registered inspectors should establish a programme of team meetings with clear agendas. Opportunities should be provided for:

i   discussion of emerging issues which require the attention of the whole team, such as the standards of oracy or writing across the curriculum, use of support staff, the effects of withdrawing pupils from lessons, or pupils' spiritual, moral, social and cultural development;

ii   the resolution of issues identified earlier as requiring a particular focus during the inspection;

iii   an exchange of information as part of each individual inspector's evidence base;

iv   discussion of any weakness or gaps in the evidence base, and how to fill them;

v   consideration of evidence which contributes to main inspection findings and key issues for action;

vi   discussion of evidence and judgements to ensure consistency, and resolution of conflicts where they arise; and

vii   consideration, as a team, of whether the school is failing or likely to fail to give its pupils an acceptable standard of education.

---

14   The Health and Safety at Work (HSW) Act 1974 places certain responsibilities on employers, which will differ according to the type of school. In county, controlled and special agreement schools the employer is the local education authority (LEA). The governing body is the employer in aided, self-governing grant-maintained schools and city technology colleges. In some independent schools the school proprietor is the employer. Inspectors should refer to the relevant edition of the DFE publication *School Governors: A Guide to the Law*.

## CORPORATE JUDGEMENTS

**75** The sharing and testing of hypotheses and evidence will inform the corporate work of the team. The registered inspector should ensure that the overall judgements about the school are shared by the inspection team. These corporate judgements can most easily be reached through discussion involving all team members towards the end of the inspection. Ultimately the registered inspector must adjudicate, if necessary, and have the final word on judgements to be included in his or her report.

## DETERMINING WHETHER A SCHOOL REQUIRES SPECIAL MEASURES[15]

**76** The criteria to be used in determining whether a school is failing or likely to fail to give its pupils an acceptable standard of education are listed in Annex 1 to Part I and should be applied carefully. The registered inspector should consider with the team whether the standards achieved and quality of education provided are so greatly impaired that many pupils are under-attaining and not receiving the education to which they are entitled, or if pupils are at a serious physical or emotional risk from adults in the school or from other pupils. A judgement that a school is failing must not be withheld on the grounds that the school's management is likely at some stage in the future to be able to improve the situation.

**77** Where the inspection team considers that the accumulating inspection evidence suggests that the school may require special measures, further guidance may be sought at any time directly from OFSTED. Once the registered inspector and team judge that special measures may be required, the registered inspector should inform the headteacher orally, before leaving the school, that in the opinion of the inspection team there are serious deficiencies and that the team is considering whether the school is failing, or likely to fail, to give its pupils an acceptable standard of education.

**78** The registered inspector must come to a judgement about whether the school requires special measures before reporting the inspection findings to senior managers and the appropriate authority and must inform OFSTED before telling the school.

**79** Where the inspection team suspects that any individual pupil is seriously at risk, action should be taken to inform the headteacher and appropriate authority immediately.

---

[15] The action set out in paragraph 23 of Part 1 of the *Framework* is that required under Section 206 (7) of the Education Act 1993.

## AFTER THE INSPECTION

### ORAL REPORTING TO THE HEADTEACHER AND THE APPROPRIATE AUTHORITY

**80**    The registered inspector, accompanied by one or more team members, must offer to discuss the inspection findings with the headteacher and any other staff of the school whom the head wishes to invite, normally the senior management team. In small schools this may, at the headteacher's discretion, involve the whole staff.

**81**    The registered inspector must also offer to meet the appropriate authority to discuss the inspection findings. This meeting is called by the appropriate authority, and its composition is determined by them **but must include the headteacher.** Nothing at the meeting of the appropriate authority should come as a surprise to the headteacher. The appropriate authority of county and voluntary schools can, if they wish, invite representatives of the LEA. The meetings with the headteacher and with the governing body must both take place before the written report is finalised.

**82**    During these meetings the registered inspector should emphasise the following:

i    oral feedback remains confidential and the findings of the inspection must not be released to the press until after the report has been received by the appropriate authority; and

ii    the school should point out any factual errors and these will be corrected in the report; judgements are not negotiable.

**83**    The quality of feedback is an important factor in influencing how the school responds to the inspection findings, particularly in drawing up its action plan, to improve any areas of weakness. Effective oral feedback:

i    is well-structured, clear, succinct, unrushed and allows opportunities for discussion and clarification; and

ii    presents a balanced, rounded picture of the work, giving credit to schools where they do things well and pinpointing any weaknesses.

**84**    Registered inspectors should also note that:

i    the purpose of the meeting is to present main findings and key issues, and to highlight key areas for action but not to advise on possible action to be taken;

ii    the meetings provide an opportunity, in covering the management and efficiency of the school, to comment on any self-evaluation or quality assurance processes undertaken by the school;

iii    the text of the schedule, Section 3.1 "Characteristics of the school" should be agreed with the headteacher and the appropriate authority; and

iv    representatives of the appropriate authority will be better able to follow what is being reported if, for the purposes of the meeting only, they are shown copies of the draft Main Findings and Key Issues for Action and if the presentation draws on visual aids. It is not necessary to read, word by word, the entire draft report.

**85** A draft report should be shown to the school to assist with the checking of factual content but not to have judgements negotiated. The draft report should not be shared in advance of the feedback to the head and appropriate authority. Factual errors identified either during meetings or from the draft report should be corrected.

## THE REPORT AND SUMMARY OF THE REPORT

**86** The report and summary of the report must communicate unequivocal judgements in straightforward language so that:

i    parents, members of the appropriate authority and the local community can have a clear understanding of the school's strengths and weaknesses: and

ii    the school has a useful basis for subsequent action.

**87** The report should reflect the individual school as it is. It must follow the structure and precise headings set out in the inspection schedule but its content, wording and style should not be written to any predetermined formula. Key judgements must be absolutely clear, and consistent with the oral report. Reasons for judgements should be given so that readers understand why the inspection team has arrived at these views. While judgements should be based on the criteria set out in the schedule, the report should focus on strengths and weaknesses. It is not necessary to allude to each and every criterion in the schedule, nor to quote the criteria, parrot-fashion.

**88** It is essential that the report makes clear the inspection team's judgements about the educational standards achieved by pupils at the school (sections 4.1 to 4.3). Overall judgements should be illustrated by reference to the strengths and weaknesses in the areas of learning or different subjects of the curriculum with particular emphasis on the core subjects.

**89** When considering the quality of education provided, inspectors must focus in particular on the quality of teaching. Other aspects of provision are important only in terms of their effect on the quality of teaching and learning, of what is provided and the educational standards achieved. Where those other aspects of provision are unexceptional, further justification is often unnecessary. Where there are particular strengths and weaknesses, though, amplification is needed to explain why, for example, mathematics teaching is 'outstanding' or leadership is 'weak.'

**90** The choice of adjective is left to the discretion of the registered inspector except that something judged 'sound' or 'satisfactory' must be better than simply strengths balanced by weaknesses. The teaching of a subject, for example, is satisfactory only if the majority of pupils make adequate progress in lessons.

**91** The 'Main Findings of Inspection' and the 'Key Issues for Action' are particularly important sections of the report. They constitute the summary of the full report but also form the basis of the summary of the report for parents. These sections need particularly careful drafting in order to communicate effectively to a wide readership. They must draw out the key judgements about the school and leave the school without any doubt about the issues which need to be tackled in order to raise the educational standards achieved and why the inspection team has identified particular issues for action. The contents of these sections of the report must be consistent with, and flow from, the body of the full report.

**92** The report, and the summary of the report, should therefore:

   i    be clear to all of its readers - the appropriate authority, parents, professionals and the wider public;

   ii   concentrate on evaluating rather than describing what is seen;

   iii  focus on the educational standards achieved and the factors which impact on standards and quality;

   iv  use everyday language, not educational jargon, and be grammatically correct;

   v   be concrete and specific;

   vi  use sub-headings and bullet points, where they help to make the message clear;

   vii  use telling examples drawn from the evidence base in order to make generalisations understandable and to illustrate what is meant by 'good' or 'poor'; and

   viii employ words and phrases that enliven the report and convey the individual character of the school.

**93** The report and summary report must be consistent with one another. Readers of the summary report will not necessarily read the full report. The summary must, therefore, be capable of standing alone as a fair and balanced picture of the school, and the steps needed to improve it.

**94** The summary must include the elements specified in the Inspection Schedule. The brief contextual statement about the school should be limited to its type and size. In addition, the summary report must include the following standard text:

■   at the beginning

"The school was inspected in (*month - year*). This is a summary of the inspector's full report, which can be obtained from the school".

■   at the end

"The governing body is responsible for drawing up an ACTION PLAN within forty working days of receiving the report, showing what the school is going to do about the issues. This action plan will be circulated to all parents at the school."

**"THE INSPECTION"**

"(*Name of school*) was inspected as part of a national programme of school inspection. The purpose is to identify strengths and weaknesses in schools that may improve the quality of education offered and raise the standards achieved by their pupils. The inspection of all schools within a four-year cycle is also designed to give parents more information about their children's schools. A copy of this summary is sent to every family with a child at the school.

The inspection of (*name of school*) took place between (*specify dates*). It was undertaken by an independent team of (*number*) inspectors, led by (*name of RgI*). The inspection was commissioned by the Office for Standards in Education, a department of central government.

The team was required to report on the **standards** achieved by pupils, the **quality of education** provided by the school, the **efficiency** with which financial resources were used and the contribution made by the school to its pupils' **spiritual, moral, social and cultural development**".

95   The report and summary report must be produced within 5 (calendar) weeks from the end of the inspection and forwarded without delay to the appropriate authority, HMCI and persons specified in Section 209 of the 1993 Act (or paragraph 9c of Schedule 2 to the 1992 Act).

96   More detailed guidance on writing the report and some examples of report sections will be provided to inspectors.

## DOCUMENTS REQUIRED BY OFSTED

97   Registered inspectors must return material to OFSTED as set out in the Contract, as follows:

- the inspection report and summary;
- text and grades in the *School Profile*;
- grades from the *Subject Profile*;
- codes and grades from the *Observation Forms*; and
- the completed *Headteacher's Form*.

All of the above material is required electronically in the format prescribed by OFSTED.

## DOCUMENTS TO BE RETAINED BY REGISTERED INSPECTORS

98   Registered inspectors are required to retain the complete *Record of Evidence* for 12 months from the date of publication of the report. As well as copies of the above, they must therefore keep the following material:

- text from *Observation Forms*, which is not routinely required by OFSTED and can be held within the *RoE* in **manuscript** form;

- text from the *Subject Profile*, which is not routinely required by OFSTED and can be held within the *RoE* in **manuscript** form;

- the *Headteacher's Statement* and PICSI Report; and

- any other evidence the registered inspector wishes to retain.

On request, inspectors must send some or all of this material to OFSTED at any time during the 12-month period after the report is published.


## SCHOOLS REQUIRING SPECIAL MEASURES

**99** Where a school is deemed to be failing or likely to fail to give its pupils an acceptable standard of education, and OFSTED has been informed of this, the registered inspector should:

i    inform the senior managers and the appropriate authority that the judgement of the team is that the school is failing, or likely to fail, to give its pupils an acceptable standard of education, and explain the reasons for this judgement. The following form of words could be used:

"I am of the opinion that special measures are required in relation to this school because it is failing (or is likely to fail) to give its pupils an acceptable standard of education. In accordance with Section 206(2) of the Education Act 1993 I shall send a draft report to HMCI and will await his judgement whether he agrees or not that this school requires special measures";

ii    explain that submission of the draft report to OFSTED may delay the issue of the report to the appropriate authority, but the maximum delay is three months from the time when the report was due; and

iii    submit to OFSTED the draft report and such other papers as are requested within five weeks of the end of the inspection.

Following receipt of the draft report, HMI from OFSTED will consider the evidence and will usually visit the school before recommending to HMCI whether or not to agree that the school requires special measures.

If HMCI agrees the judgement, the registered inspector must state this in the report and summary of the report. The following form of words should be used:

"In accordance with Section 206(7) of the Education Act 1993[16], I am of the opinion, and HMCI agrees, that special measures are required in relation to this school."

If HMCI does not agree, OFSTED will discuss available options with the registered inspector.

---

[16]    In the case of independent schools (including city technology colleges and city colleges for the technology of the arts) use "In accordance with paragraph 9 of Schedule 2 of the 1992 Education (Schools) Act as amended by paragraph 173 of Schedule 19 to the 1993 Act ..."

# PART III

# THE INSPECTION SCHEDULE AND GUIDANCE ON ITS USE

## THE STRUCTURE OF THE SCHEDULE

■ This section provides guidance for all inspectors on the use of the inspection schedule which is set out in the *Framework*. The schedule is the key to producing a report which evaluates the school accurately and informatively.

■ The diagram below shows the structure of the schedule, and hence the inspection report. It highlights the distinction between *outcomes*, with an emphasis on attainment and progress, and the *factors which contribute to these outcomes*, particularly teaching.

### CONTEXT

3.1 Characteristics of the School

### OUTCOMES

| Educational standards achieved | 4.2 Attitudes, behaviour & personal development | 4.1 Attainment & progress | 4.3 Attendance | |
|---|---|---|---|---|

### CONTRIBUTORY FACTORS

| Provision | 5.2 The curriculum & assessment | 5.3 Pupils' spiritual moral, social & cultural development | 5.1 Teaching | 5.4 Support, guidance & pupils' welfare | 5.5 Partnership with parents & the community |
|---|---|---|---|---|---|
| Management | 6.2 Staffing, accommodation & learning resources | | 6.1 Leadership & management | 6.3 The efficiency of the school | |

In using each section of the schedule, inspectors should have regard for what is achieved by and provided for *all* pupils in the school, whatever their age, attainment, gender, background, ethnicity or special educational need.

The inspection findings should be set in the context of the school and its own aims and priorities for development. This background is established in Section 3.1.

## OUTCOMES

■ **Educational standards achieved by pupils** are covered in three sections.

♦ *Attainment and progress* focuses on the first priority of inspection: to determine what pupils know, understand and can do, and how this compares with national standards or expectations; and to evaluate their progress.

♦ *Attitudes, behaviour and personal development* constitutes pupils' response to what the school offers through its teaching and other provision.

♦ *Attendance* – including punctuality – reflects another kind of response to school.

Inspection reports should concentrate in these sections on judgements about outcomes, as distinct from the quality of what is provided and other contributory factors.

## CONTRIBUTORY FACTORS

■ **Provision, or the quality of education provided,** is covered in five sections, and should be evaluated in terms of its contribution to the outcomes.

♦ *Teaching* is the major factor contributing to pupils' attainment, progress and response. Thorough evaluation of its quality and its impact on the educational standards achieved by pupils is, therefore, central to inspection.

*Reporting on the rest of these sections should concentrate on strengths and weaknesses, illustrating the judgements with examples drawn from the evidence base. Where the aspect concerned is satisfactory or unexceptional, only a brief evaluation is needed.*

♦ *The curriculum and assessment* involves evaluation of how the school provides and assesses a full range of learning experiences in order to promote the attainment, progress and personal development of all pupils.

♦ *The spiritual, moral, social and cultural development of pupils* is concerned with four aspects of personal development in which schools have an important part to play.

♦ *Support, guidance and pupils' welfare* focuses on the provision the school makes to enable all pupils to take full advantage of the educational opportunities offered, to feel secure and to have high but realistic expectations of themselves.

♦ *Partnership with parents and the community* explores the links which can strengthen the support and guidance of pupils, enrich curricular opportunities and help pupils to progress.

These sections focus on different aspects of provision but are interrelated. They draw largely from the same body of evidence: the school's documentation; the views of parents; observation of work in classrooms and other activities; scrutiny of pupils' work; and discussions with pupils, governors, headteacher and staff.

■ **The management and efficiency of the school** is covered in three sections which are closely connected:

- ◆ *Leadership and management* is concerned with the educational standards set, the quality of provision and the monitoring and evaluation undertaken to promote and sustain their improvement.

- ◆ *Staffing, accommodation and learning resources* is concerned with the adequacy of the school's resources and their impact on standards and quality.

- ◆ *The efficiency of the school* calls for a summative judgement on the use the school makes of its available resources to achieve the best possible outcomes for all its pupils.

## SUBJECTS AND COURSES

■ Evaluation of pupils' attainment and progress and the school's provision for the subjects and courses of the curriculum is at the heart of the inspection process. It forms the basis for judging the educational standards of the school and provides much of the evidence about the quality of provision, particularly teaching, as well as the impact of the management and efficiency of the school.

## REPORTING

■ Collecting and analysing evidence means that the same issues are often seen from different perspectives. The registered inspector should avoid duplication or repetition when writing the report. One example is assessment, aspects of which relate to teaching, the curriculum and partnership with parents.

■ The **Main Findings** of the report must highlight educational standards, but they provide the opportunity to show links between outcomes, provision and management. The main findings must incorporate evaluation of the four statutory areas to be reported, identifying major strengths and weaknesses. The **Key Issues for Action** should draw from the main findings to provide a basis on which the school can act.

## THE STRUCTURE OF THE GUIDANCE

■ The sections follow a common pattern. Each page from the *Framework schedule* is matched by *guidance* which includes the following elements.

The **inspection focus** highlights the central judgements which **must** be made. It provides an interpretation of those parts of the schedule which define what inspectors must evaluate and report on. Inspectors must be clear about the judgements to be made to give purpose and direction to the gathering and interpretation of evidence.

**Using the criteria** illustrates how the criteria should be interpreted and how the evidence is tested against them. The criteria amount to standards for good practice. They provide inspectors with a basis for accurate and consistent evaluation and for the identification of strengths and weaknesses. In reaching overall judgements, all the relevant criteria should be considered.

The criteria can be used in different ways. On the one hand, they can be used to test and check an initial view or hypothesis, for example, that the observed teaching is very good. Alternatively, they can be used cumulatively to build up an overall judgement, for example about the curriculum.

*Guidance on using the criteria is provided as a source of reference and not as a prescription to be followed. In using the guidance it is important for the inspection team to focus on the central judgements required by the Framework and not to pursue such a diverse range of issues that the inspection becomes unmanageable.*

In reporting, inspectors should avoid simply quoting criteria and should concentrate on the reporting requirements highlighted in the schedule. Evidence needs to be drawn into the report to illustrate judgements, bring the report to life and capture the individual characteristics of the school.

The summary of **main sources of evidence** outlines the key evidence to be collected and analysed before and during the inspection to enable the central judgements to be made.

**Additional notes** provide guidance where necessary on particular issues covered in the schedule.

**Inspection schedule**

## 1 Main Findings

The "Main Findings" (Section 1) together with the "Key Issues for Action" (Section 2) will be included in the summary report which is distributed to parents. These sections must be written in a clear and comprehensible style appropriate for this readership.

### THE REPORT MUST INCLUDE

- a summary of the main inspection judgements on the educational standards achieved in the school.

- an evaluation of the school's effectiveness in promoting high standards through the quality of education provided, concentrating in particular upon the quality of teaching, and including the spiritual, moral, social and cultural development of pupils, and the efficiency with which the school's resources are managed.

Where a school is judged to be failing or likely to fail to give its pupils an acceptable standard of education and therefore requires special measures, this must be stated[17].

Where a school has previously been inspected under Section 9 or Section 3(1) of the 1992 Act, the report should give the date of the previous inspection and should summarise the steps taken by the school to implement the action plan which resulted from the inspection.

---

17   As required by the 1992 Act and amended by Section 206(7) of the 1993 Act.

## Guidance on using the schedule

### INSPECTION FOCUS

■ The main findings should reflect the essential characteristics and qualities of the school. They should focus on the educational standards achieved by pupils and the strengths and weaknesses in the quality of education provided, especially teaching, and on the management and efficiency of the school as they affect the standards.

The main findings should incorporate summary judgements on the four reporting requirements:

◆ the educational standards achieved by pupils in the school;

◆ the quality of education provided;

◆ the spiritual, moral, social and cultural development of pupils; and

◆ the efficiency with which the financial resources made available to the school are managed.

As well as pointing clearly to significant areas in need of improvement, the opportunity should also be taken to highlight what the school does particularly well.

Where a school is judged to be failing, or likely to fail, to give its pupils an acceptable standard of education, this must be stated in the main findings. The form of words which must be used is given in Part II of the *Handbook*.

If a school has previously been inspected under Section 9 or subsequently under Section 3(1) of the 1992 Act, the main findings should conclude with an evaluative comment on the extent to which issues identified in the previous inspection have been addressed. The summary should state how well the school has responded to the previous inspection, indicating those issues on which significant progress has been made and any outstanding matters which need attention.

**Inspection schedule**

## 2 Key Issues for Action

### THE REPORT MUST INCLUDE

■ a list of the specific matters which the appropriate authority for the school must address in constructing its action plan.

The **key issues for action** should draw from the **main findings** and focus on the most significant weaknesses identified in the inspection, particularly in relation to pupils' attainment and progress and the quality of education provided, with particular emphasis on teaching. They are likely to be few in number and should provide a clear and practicable basis on which the appropriate authority and school can act.

Details of any non-compliance with statutory requirements should be included where they detract significantly from the quality and standards of the school, together with any significant concerns about health and safety.

The key issues should be given in an order of priority which reflects their importance in improving pupils' attainment. Where the inspection highlights issues already identified as priorities in the school's development plan, this section should make reference to the fact.

**Guidance on using the schedule**

## INSPECTION FOCUS

■ The key issues identified by the inspection will form the basis of the school's action plan. It is important, therefore, that the key issues:

◆ derive from the main findings;

◆ are clear, precise and specific to the school;

◆ provide a practical basis for identifiable improvements in the educational standards achieved by pupils.

The order of priority should reflect the significance of the issues in contributing to the educational standards achieved by pupils, with an emphasis on matters which can realistically be addressed and progress made within, for example, the year following the inspection. This order of priority should be explained during feedback.

There is no need to manufacture these issues in very effective schools where there are no significant weaknesses.

The registered inspector should ensure that the implications of the issues raised are fully understood by the headteacher and governors, and that the issues are expressed unequivocally in the report. For example, "the curriculum needs to be reviewed in mathematics" is no substitute for "to raise attainment and improve mathematical understanding at Key Stages 2 and 3, pupils need more regular practice in using number in practical situations."

Mention should also be made of any provision or practice noted during the inspection which, in the opinion of the inspectors, may constitute a significant breach of the law or a serious threat to health and safety. Compliance with statutory requirements is covered in Section 6.1. Guidance on health and safety is given in the commentary on Section 5.4.

**Inspection schedule**

## 3 Introduction

### 3.1 CHARACTERISTICS OF THE SCHOOL

**THE REPORT MUST INCLUDE**

- a concise factual statement about the characteristics of the school and its pupils and the area it serves.

The statement should include the number of pupils on roll, the number of pupils identified as having special educational needs and a description of the composition of the school in terms of pupils' attainment on entry, gender, ethnicity and background.

- a brief statement of the main aims and priorities of the school, including any targets set by the school.

The text of Section 3.1 should be agreed with the headteacher and the appropriate authority.

**Guidance on using the schedule**

## INSPECTION FOCUS

■ This section should briefly describe the school in a way which provides relevant information as a background to the inspection report, limited where possible to two paragraphs.

The first paragraph should state the characteristics listed in the inspection schedule. The statement should include a description of the nature of disabilities for which the school provides. This may be different from the school's designated approval. The registered inspector and the appropriate authority may, however, agree to include in this paragraph other features which are significant to the inspection, for example, a recent major change in roll, recent changes in the character of the school and any integration or college links. The main sources of evidence are the PICSI report, the *Headteacher's Form* and *Statement* and the discussion which takes place with the headteacher and appropriate authority.

The second paragraph should capture what the school sees as its main aims and priorities. Particular mention should be made of any targets, related to educational standards, which the school has set. The school's aims and priorities will be drawn from the prospectus, the school development plan and from discussion.

It is particularly important to ensure that the headteacher and appropriate authority agree that the second paragraph accurately reflects the school's main aims, priorities and targets.

Evaluation of the relevance of the aims, priorities and targets, and of how they have been pursued, should be reported in Section 6.1.

The registered inspector must decide whether it is appropriate to make judgements about achievement in relation to the expectation of what most pupils attain. If the decision, as in most special schools, is to make a judgement solely against pupils' past attainment and their capability, the registered inspector must make this clear in this section of the report.

**Inspection schedule**

## 3.2 KEY INDICATORS[18]

■ The report should include indicators which summarise the attainment of pupils at the end of each key stage, together with comparative performance data where these are available.

Depending on the time of the inspection, national data may or may not refer to the same school year. The years to which the data refer should be clearly stated.

**At the end of Key Stage 1:**

Proportion of pupils attaining level 2 or above in specified subjects or attainment targets.

**At the end of Key Stage 2:**

Proportion of pupils attaining level 4 or above in specified subjects or attainment targets.

**At the end of Key Stage 3:**

Proportion of pupils attaining levels 5 and above, and 6 and above, in specified subjects or attainment targets.

**At the end of Key Stage 4 and post-16:**

Comparative attainment data from the annual performance tables.

■ The report should include school and comparative national attendance data, showing the percentages of half-days missed through authorised and through unauthorised absence.

School exclusion data should show the numbers of fixed-term and permanent exclusions of pupils of compulsory school age during the previous school year.

OFSTED will from time to time provide registered inspectors and contractors with a current specification of data to be included in the report.

■ The report should also state the percentage of teaching observed in the school as a whole which was: very good or better; satisfactory or better; and less than satisfactory.

---

18 Where the Rgl has decided to judge achievement against national norms, this section should be included. For schools where the pupils' attainment is judged solely against their individual progress and capability, comparative data should be omitted but details of any successes in nationally accredited courses and a summary of end-of-key stage tests should be recorded.

**Guidance on using the schedule**

## INSPECTION FOCUS

■ If a decision has been taken to report on attainment in relation to national expectations (see Inspection Focus, page 55), this section should include a summary of the attainment of pupils at the end of each key stage and for post-16 students. It is often inappropriate, however, to compare the results of a special school with others of the same type, because of the wide ability range within schools, the differences in identification procedures, and the variation in policies for special educational needs across LEAs.

The report should present the school's data clearly and concisely, together with comparative data provided by OFSTED, where this is relevant. The format of presentation is, however, left to the registered inspector, whose aim should be to make the data as clear as possible to a lay readership.

No data below KS1 is required in this section of the report. The attainment data required are drawn from those which are published for parents, or those in annual performance tables. The registered inspector is responsible for compiling this data as specified for the report. Other data for this section of the report can be taken directly from the *Headteacher's Form*.

The data on the proportion of teaching which is very good or better, satisfactory or better and less than satisfactory should be compiled from the observation of teaching. Very good teaching is summarised as grades 1 and 2 on the 7-point scale; satisfactory or better as grades 1 to 4; and less than satisfactory as grades 5 to 7.

Details of the grading scale are given in the *Inspection Resource Pack*.

**Inspection schedule**

# PART A: ASPECTS OF THE SCHOOL

## 4 Educational standards achieved by pupils at the school

### 4.1 ATTAINMENT AND PROGRESS

*Inspectors must evaluate and report on what pupils achieve by 5 in nursery or reception classes, by the end of each key stage and by 19, with reference, where appropriate, to:*

■ attainment;

i   in the school overall, in relation to national standards or expectations, highlighting any significant variations in attainment among pupils of different gender, ethnicity or background;

ii   in English, mathematics and science, and in the other subjects or areas inspected, highlighting relative strengths and weaknesses;

iii   over time, if there are any clear trends in overall attainment, with a comment on how well any targets set or adopted by the school are being met.

■ progress in relation to prior attainment.

*Judgements should be based on the extent to which:*

◆ the attainment of pupils at the end of nursery education or by five in reception classes meets or exceeds expectations for their age;

◆ the attainment of pupils at 7, 11, 14 and 16 years meets or exceeds national standards, particularly in English, mathematics and science;

◆ students by 19 years achieve or exceed two GCE A-level passes or equivalent[19]; and leave school with qualifications relevant to the next stage of education or training, or employment;

◆ pupils with special educational needs progress as well as or better than expected;

◆ the attainment and progress of minority groups of pupils is comparable with others in the school;

◆ the school sustains high levels of attainment or is improving.

---

[19]   For example, advanced GNVQ.

## Guidance on using the schedule

### INSPECTION FOCUS

■ The main priorities of inspection are to *assess* what pupils know, understand and can do (their attainment) to *evaluate* pupils' progress in relation to their prior attainment. This represents the pupils' achievement.

The registered inspector will need to make a decision at the outset of the inspection about whether it is appropriate to report judgements in relation to national standards or expectations.

In some special schools where the whole of the ability range is represented, pupils' attainments may be compared to national expectations. Pupils' attainments in these circumstances may represent achievements which deserve highlighting, and inspectors should report on this. In most special schools the nature of the pupils' learning difficulties is such that it would not be appropriate or reasonable to compare attainment to national expectations.

In all special schools, judgements will centre on pupils' progress. The judgements should be made, after considering pupils' attainment and capabilities. This is indicated by information contained in the advice within statements of special educational need, in annual reviews, teachers' planning such as individual education plans (IEPs) and records, as well as from inspectors' observations and discussions.

As described in 3.1 and 3.2, it is not possible to make valid comparisons about achievement between special schools serving similar types of special need because of the diversity of intake from one school or LEA to another, within the same LEA, and the very different ability profile.

Inspectors will need to explain the context against which judgements on attainmentt are made, for example:

i    by making sure the intake profile is adequately described;

ii   by explaining when attainment is judged to be less than it could be despite recent good progress (for example, after a recent admission);

iii  by explaining where for some pupils there may be important factors that affect progress, and in some cases result in regression.

### USING THE CRITERIA

The criteria should be applied wherever relevant to the type of special school being inspected.

*Does the attainment of pupils at the end of nursery education or by five in reception classes meet or exceed expectations for their age?*

## Guidance on using the schedule

■ Many pupils leave nursery provision soon after they are four years old to enter reception classes, usually after 3 or 4 terms in nursery education. Some may have started to read, write and count, while others may not yet have acquired these skills. Where a school has a nursery class or unit, the judgement of attainment should consider the children under five as a whole, both in nursery and reception classes, but focus in particular on the attainment of pupils by five.[20]

### *Does the attainment of pupils at 7, 11, 14 and 16 years meet or exceed national standards, particularly in English, mathematics and science?*

■ The emphasis on English, mathematics and science reflects the importance of these core subjects in the National Curriculum. Judgements at KS1 and KS2 should take into account the school's results in the end-of-key stage tests and teacher assessments. These must be set in the context of national comparative data, the interpretation of which will develop over time and will be communicated by OFSTED. At KS4, judgements of attainment should take into account performance in all GCSE or other accreditation. However, at all key stages, inspectors need to go beyond test results and teacher assessments as these invariably apply to pupils who have moved into a new year group or who have left the school. These results do not give the complete picture.

In relation to English and mathematics, inspectors should draw on evidence from across the curriculum. They should consider whether the essential skills of these subjects, ie reading, writing, speaking, listening and the use of number, are sufficiently developed to enhance learning across the curriculum or whether the levels of such skills are too low and are a barrier to progress.

Inspectors should report strengths and weaknesses in attainment for pupils at 7, 11, 14 and 16 in the other subjects or courses inspected. Evidence should include pupils' work, discussion and observation. This will be especially important in those subjects for which test data is limited or unavailable. In these cases, inspectors should base their judgements on their knowledge of the average range of attainment for pupils at these ages.

### *Do students by 19 years achieve or exceed two GCE A-level passes or the equivalent and leave school with qualifications relevant to the next stage of education or training?*

■ Attainment by students post-16 should be judged taking account of the criteria, including the grade or performance criteria, for the course being followed. Inspectors should use national average grades, point scores or pass rates for the subjects or courses concerned, to set the performance of students in the school in context. They should take account of the difference in assessment regimes between vocational courses such as GNVQ, which are criterion-referenced, and other examinations with aggregated forms of assessment, such as GCSE and A/AS-level. Inspectors should also take account of the destinations of school leavers.

There are some general features of attainment post-16 which can be used to guide evaluation across a range of courses:

◆ a secure grasp of relevant specialist knowledge and its application;

---

[20] Guidance is available in OFSTED's occasional paper for inspectors pending the development of agreed national guidelines for the education of the under-fives, but may not apply to some pupils with SEN.

- the development of intellectual skills and a capacity to be innovative in their use;

- higher-level experimental and investigational skills;

- the ability to analyse, interpret and critically evaluate material from a variety of sources;

- the ability to construct and express, both orally and in writing, relevant, coherent and cogent explanation and argument;

- the ability to interpret data in a variety of forms and, when appropriate, make predictions or formulate hypotheses and test them;

- the development of individual strategies for the management and completion of tasks, in preparation for effective progression to continuing education, training or employment.

*Do pupils progress as well as or better than expected?*

*Is the attainment of minority groups of pupils comparable with others in the school?*

■ All pupils in a special school have a special educational need. Judgements about progress in general draw from evaluation of the progress of individual pupils.

These two criteria call for evaluation of the progress pupils make: their *gains* in knowledge, understanding and skills. Analysis depends on comparing current with prior attainment.

It is possible for pupils having above-average attainment to make unsatisfactory progress because it is not as good as expected in relation to their prior attainment. Conversely, pupils with very low attainment may make better than expected progress even though eventual attainment still falls short of the average for their age.

Evidence of progress should come from the following sources:

- the main reference points are the statement, the last annual review, and targets for improvement within the individual education plan;

- observation of pupils at work provides evidence of new learning or the application and extension of previous learning over a short timescale – that is, within a lesson or sequence of lessons;

- in KS1 it is increasingly common to be able to refer to 'baseline assessments', i.e. profiles of pupils on entry, to provide evidence of prior attainment;

- in KS2 inspectors should refer to KS1 tests and assessments;

- progress in KS4 can be checked against the results of earlier key stage tests and teacher assessments;

- progress of post-16 students through the subject or course can be traced in relation to earlier GCSE or other accreditation, and some schools will be in a position to provide a detailed analysis of their progress through the accreditation system;

- where appropriate, samples of pupils' earlier work should be reviewed in the light of current work to assess progress made;

## Guidance on using the schedule

◆ reference to teachers' individual records, pupil records (including records of achievement) and reports to parents can together give a detailed picture of prior attainment, targets for improvement and progress made;

◆ discussion with pupils about what they are doing, what they have learned and what they are going to do next can be illuminating;

◆ rates of progress may not be the same in all subjects or areas of learning and it is important for the team to evaluate any significant variations and to identify the reasons for them. Similarly, progress across the curriculum may be enhanced by specific progress in areas related to a pupil's special educational need (for example, behaviour, mobility, social skills).

It is important to examine the progress of different groups of pupils – for example, the different sexes, or pupils from minority ethnic backgrounds. Some schools provide more effectively for some groups than for others and inspectors need to highlight significant variations and the reasons for them. Inspectors should enquire whether the school monitors the performance of different groups and, if so, what the data reveals and how the school responds.

### Is the school sustaining high levels of attainment or improving?

■ Evidence of relatively high standards, or sustained improvement or decline over several years, should be reported. A judgement should only be made where there is solid evidence of a trend in performance, up or down, over three or four years.

Some schools set quantitative targets for improvement at school, key stage or subject level and monitor progress towards such targets. Inspectors should consider whether the targets set are appropriate and achievable, and how well they are met.

**Guidance on using the schedule**

## MAIN SOURCES OF EVIDENCE

### Before the inspection

◆ **National Curriculum assessments,** both test results and teacher assessment;

◆ **PICSI report** if provided;

◆ **evidence of attainment,** provided by the school, including entry profiles or baseline assessment; value added analysis of the progress made by pupils in a year group based on prior attainment, and the outcomes of diagnostic tests; and previous school records.

### During the inspection

The team should gather evidence of the current and prior attainment of pupils throughout the school including:

◆ **teacher assessments and records;**

◆ **observation of pupils at work** to give evidence of both attainment and progress;

◆ **scrutiny of samples of pupils' current and earlier work,** including records of National Curriculum assessments and other teacher assessments;

◆ **analysis of individual education plans, statements and annual reviews** for a sample of pupils;

◆ **discussions** with pupils and staff provide valuable insights into the pupils' knowledge and understanding of the work in hand and the progress they have made.

## 4.2 ATTITUDES, BEHAVIOUR AND PERSONAL DEVELOPMENT

*Inspectors must evaluate and report on pupils' response to the teaching and other provision made by the school, highlighting strengths and weaknesses, as shown by:*

■ their attitudes to learning;

■ their behaviour, including incidence of exclusions;

■ the quality of relationships in the school including the degree of racial harmony, where applicable;

■ other aspects of their personal development, including their contributions to the life of the community.

*Judgements should be based on the extent to which pupils:*

◆ show interest in their work and are able to sustain concentration and develop their capacity for personal study;

◆ behave well in and around the school, and are courteous and trustworthy and show respect for property;

◆ form constructive relationships with one another, with teachers and other adults, and work collaboratively when required;

◆ show respect for other people's feelings, values and beliefs;

◆ show initiative and are willing to take responsibility.

**Guidance on using the schedule**

## INSPECTION FOCUS

■ This section is concerned with how pupils respond to school in terms of their attitudes to learning, their behaviour and their values and personal development. The criteria cover the pupils' response to the school's provision, particularly teaching, the curriculum, and provision for spiritual, moral, social and cultural development.

■ Good communication with parents is the basis for productive attitudes to learning, good behaviour and positive personal development. Pupils' attitudes have a significant bearing on their attainment and progress and can be strongly influenced by what schools do. For young children, their first experiences of school are extremely important in developing positive attitudes to learning.

Good behaviour is vital. If pupils are to benefit from the teaching, the class and school must function as an orderly community. How pupils behave in and around the school is a reflection of their attitude and personal development, evidence of which will also be seen in their classroom work and other activities through, for example, a growing ability to respect other people and their views. An important feature is how well the school manages arrangements for promoting respect for self and for others, and acceptance of rules and conventions that will enhance the quality of pupils' life in and out of school.

A high priority in special schools is the personal development of pupils towards attaining independence and autonomy, personal fulfilment and achievement, and the development of social skills and formation of effective relationships. The particular emphasis given will reflect pupils' special educational needs, and responses will be expected to be observable across the whole curriculum.

Definitions of aspects of personal development are given in Section 5.3.

■ Overall judgements should identify the strengths and weaknesses in pupils' attitudes to learning. On the basis of the team's observations in lessons and around the school, inspectors should judge pupils' behaviour and its effect on their learning and on the school. A judgement should also be made on the basis of all the evidence available about the overall quality of pupils' personal development.

Pupils' attitudes to learning and levels of interest will depend upon the particular needs related to their disability and on the competence of staff in employing essential specialist teaching/support approaches which engage the pupils actively in their learning. Pupil levels and lengths of concentration and motivation will, therefore, vary significantly across and within age groups at pre-5, each key stage and post-16.

Some pupils with special educational needs have experienced significant difficulties in behaviour and motivation before entering the school. Inspectors should look for the development, from a low baseline, of positive attitudes to learning, good behaviour and personal responsibility.

**Guidance on using the schedule**

## USING THE CRITERIA

*Do pupils show interest in their work? Are they able to sustain concentration and extend their capacity for personal study?*

■ Inspectors should look for evidence of pupils' involvement in and enjoyment of learning, their willingness to apply themselves to the task in hand, respond to challenging tasks, to learn from mistakes, to ask and answer questions, join in discussion and show enthusiasm.

Important evidence should emerge from discussion with pupils about whether they enjoy their work, what they find easy or difficult; how they tackle new work, what they think of their contributions in lessons and how well they are developing an understanding of their strengths and weaknesses. For younger children the main evidence will come from observing how actively they are engaged in handling and exploring equipment and materials, as well as noticing whether children stay with an activity or flit between several.

A positive approach to work is shown in:

◆ their concentration while listening to the teacher;

◆ how confidently pupils can generate ideas and solve problems;

◆ their capacity to persevere and complete tasks when difficulties arise;

◆ their ability to select and use relevant resources;

◆ their desire to improve their work and their pride in the finished product.

There should be evidence of older pupils and students carrying more responsibility for the organisation of their work, taking the initiative and setting some of their own tasks in discussion with their teachers.

In reaching a judgement, inspectors will need to consider pupils' attitudes to learning across the curriculum and in different learning contexts. The degree and type of responses will depend on their particular disabilities and will vary significantly across and within age groups. Inspectors will need to take account of factors which positively promote or inhibit pupils' attitudes to learning before making a judgement about their interest, concentration, and ability to work collaboratively and independently.

*How well do pupils behave in and around the school? Are they courteous and trustworthy? Do they show respect for property?*

*Do pupils form constructive relationships with one another, with teachers and other adults, and do they work collaboratively when required?*

■ Most of the evidence available for use when judging behaviour and relationships in the school is derived from observation of pupils at work and play. Evidence collected in relation to Section 5.1 will be central. The analysis should also take into account the views of the headteacher, staff, governors, pupils and parents. In particular, the meeting with parents should explore their perceptions of behaviour, the information they receive about rewards and sanctions and the extent to which their children are happy and confident at school.

In classrooms the main issue is whether pupils' behaviour helps their learning or obstructs it. Outside classrooms, inspectors should observe how well pupils respond to the school's rules and conventions. There are significant weaknesses in behaviour when teachers or support staff spend an undue amount of time seeking to establish discipline and maintain order.

Inspectors will need to observe pupils and talk with both them and staff to assess whether there is any inappropriate behaviour. Observation of behaviour and discussion with pupils and teachers will show the extent to which pupils know right from wrong and take responsibility for their own actions.

Inspectors should look for evidence of:

◆ ways in which pupils, including those of different ethnic groups, relate to one another;

◆ any inappropriate behaviour, including harassment or bullying, by or towards particular groups of pupils;

◆ pupils' ability to work together in lessons and to support one another in other school activities;

◆ the level of respect between pupils and teachers and other adults in school, and whether pupils are encouraged to articulate their own views and beliefs;

◆ the way pupils treat the school's and other people's property.

The number of, and the reasons for, exclusions from the school, both permanent and fixed-term, should be considered. If exclusions occur inspectors should establish whether correct procedures are followed, whether the exclusions are monitored with regard to gender and ethnicity and what patterns emerge.

### *Do pupils show respect for other people's feelings, values and beliefs?*

■ Evidence comes from observation of pupils at work, at play, and in other school activities and from discussion with pupils and staff. It includes:

◆ pupils' perceptiveness, their willingness to listen to what others in the school have to say and their interest in views and ideas different from their own;

◆ their recognition and increasing understanding of the diversity of beliefs, attitudes and social and cultural traditions;

◆ their capacity to reflect on and discuss their behaviour, feelings and experiences.

## Guidance on using the schedule

*Do pupils show initiative? Are they willing to take responsibility?*

■ This entails looking at pupils' involvement in the daily routines of the school, and their response to teaching and the curriculum. Inspectors should observe whether pupils offer to help; whether they see what needs to be done; whether they assist other pupils; whether they have particular responsibilities in the school or in the classroom. Inspectors should consider if there is increasing scope for pupils to take responsibility and show initiative as they become older, or to begin to adjust or overcome the effects of their disability. Evidence may come from discussion with staff and from talking to a sample of pupils of differing ages throughout the school.

The key is how pupils respond to the opportunities offered – for example, in presenting assemblies, putting on performances, running clubs, taking part in charitable events, arranging activities for community groups, helping in the library or the IT centre, being involved in mini-enterprises, helping to supervise younger pupils, working with them on their reading – and so on.

## Guidance on using the schedule

## MAIN SOURCES OF EVIDENCE

### Before the inspection

◆ the **school prospectus** and other information to parents may describe the attitudes, behaviour and personal developments the school is seeking to promote;

◆ **discussion at pre-inspection meetings** with the headteacher, governors and parents, and scrutiny of the completed parents' questionnaire, should provide a range of perspectives on pupils' response to school;

◆ the **school's policy on behaviour and discipline** will outline the school's strategies for encouraging a positive response from pupils.

### During the inspection

A view on how pupils respond, behave and develop can be formed through:

◆ **observation of pupils** at work and play, their participation in extra-curricular activities and contribution to the life of the school;

◆ **observation of interaction** between pupils, staff and other adults;

◆ **discussion with pupils, teaching, care and support staff** (including staff responsible for lunchtime supervision), **visiting specialists and education social workers**, exploring the extent to which the school promotes positive attitudes;

◆ **scrutiny of records** of behaviour and sanctions, including exclusions, and analysis of the nature and patterns of any poor behaviour. This will include written communication between care staff and teachers where a school makes residential provision.

## Inspection schedule

## 4.3 ATTENDANCE

### INSPECTORS MUST EVALUATE AND REPORT ON

- pupils' attendance and punctuality, analysing reasons for absence where attendance is poor or where patterns of absence affect particular groups of pupils.

*Judgements should be based on the extent to which:*

- pupils' attendance exceeds 90% and they come to school and lessons on time.

**Guidance on using the schedule**

## INSPECTION FOCUS

■ Evaluation should focus on the level of pupils' attendance and its effect on attainment and progress. Section 5.4 covers the action that the school takes.

■ Attendance for pupils under 5 or over 16 years is not a statutory requirement. Attendance for the great majority will be regular, but the attendance of some pupils may be intermittent and for others it may be interrupted by long periods of illness, medical treatment or other causes. Unauthorised absence and internal truancy may be a feature in a few schools.

Where a school makes provision for post-16 students, there should be a policy on attendance for the students who are registered which may include a statement on the use of independent study time.

The overall judgement should indicate any significant features of pupils' attendance and punctuality and comment on the effect on their attainment and progress.

## USING THE CRITERIA

*Does pupils' attendance exceed 90% and do they come to school and lessons on time?*

■ Where attendance falls below 90% for the school, an analysis of patterns of absence and their effect on attainment and progress needs to be undertaken. This analysis may show whether poor attendance or punctuality affects particular groups of pupils. Discussion with the staff and the school's education welfare officer may help to illuminate the patterns and causes of absence.

## MAIN SOURCES OF EVIDENCE

**Before the inspection**
◆ the *Headteacher's Form* gives data on pupils' attendance;
◆ the **staff handbook** may include a policy on attendance;
◆ the **PICSI** report (if available);
◆ **pre-inspection meetings** with the headteacher, and parents, may raise issues of attendance patterns.

**During the inspection**
◆ **scrutiny of registers** will confirm compliance with statutory requirements and indicate any significant patterns of absence and **registration periods** should be sampled;
◆ **transport arrangements** at the beginning and end of the day;
◆ **observation of lessons** should record the total of pupils present alongside the number on the class register, and any delays or disruption caused by lateness should be noted;
◆ **discussions** with staff and the education welfare officer, if practicable, should explore the extent to which attendance and punctuality affect teaching, attainment and progress.

**Inspection schedule**

## 5  Quality of education provided

### 5.1  TEACHING

**INSPECTORS MUST EVALUATE AND REPORT ON**

■ the quality of teaching and its contribution to pupils' attainment and progress, highlighting:

i overall strengths and weaknesses in teaching pupils under 5, in each key stage, and in the different subjects or areas of learning inspected;

ii factors which account for effective and ineffective teaching;

iii the extent to which teaching promotes the learning of all pupils.

*Judgements should be based on the extent to which teachers[21]:*

◆ have a secure knowledge and understanding of the subjects or areas they teach;

◆ set high expectations so as to challenge pupils and deepen their knowledge and understanding;

◆ plan effectively;

◆ employ methods and organisational strategies which match curricular objectives and the needs of all pupils;

◆ manage pupils well and achieve high standards of discipline;

◆ use time and resources effectively;

◆ assess pupils' work thoroughly and constructively, and use assessments to inform teaching;

◆ use homework effectively to reinforce and/or extend what is learned in school.

---

21 Or other staff involved in teaching, instruction or providing support for learning.

**Guidance on using the schedule**

## INSPECTION FOCUS

■ Teaching is the major factor contributing to pupils' attainment, progress and response. Evaluation of the quality and impact of teaching is central to inspection. Assessment is integral to the teaching process; this section covers teachers' formative day-to-day assessment, while Section 5.2 deals with the school's arrangements for assessment and recording and Section 5.5 with reporting to parents.

■ Teachers may be expected to teach a number of subjects, courses and areas of learning and demonstrate expertise in meeting the needs of the particular disabilities served. Specialist subject teaching is increasingly more likely in Key Stages 3 and 4 and with post-16 students. Teachers' command of the subject and the teaching methods and strategies they employ should be appropriate to the relevant key stage or course and the needs of pupils and students. There is likely to be increased flexibility in methods and organisation with older pupils and especially in post-16 provision – for example, through the use of coursework assignments, research tasks and off-site work.

Teachers' planning will cover areas of learning and subjects. In many instances it will need to take account of the wide range of needs in a group and the fact that some pupils will be in a mixed age class. Teachers' planning will take many different forms but its effectiveness will depend on the clarity of the objectives set for learning derived from assessment information.

Teaching methods will vary across and within special schools. They will be influenced by the capabilities of the pupils, their stage of development and the outcomes of reviews, IEPs and inputs from therapists. Teaching methods must suit the area of learning or subject as well as the pupils; essentially the use of any particular strategy is to ensure that pupils are provided with suitably attainable challenges.

The management of time and resources to support pupils individually, in groups, or when they receive therapy outside the classroom setting, is a challenge to both pupils and adults in the special school. In particular, the task is to ensure that time is used effectively and that pupils receive a cohesive, broad and balanced programme in which their specific special needs are also addressed.

■ Overall judgements about teaching will derive from those made in each lesson or session observed, covering the subjects or areas of learning and all year groups in the school. Pupils' work provides supplementary evidence. The report should include illustrations of successful and less successful teaching methods.

**Guidance on using the schedule**

## USING THE CRITERIA

*Do teachers have a secure knowledge and understanding of the subjects or areas they teach?*

■ The assessment of teachers' subject expertise begins with their knowledge and understanding of the National Curriculum subject Orders, the relevant syllabus for religious education, the areas of learning for pupils under five and course and examination requirements at KS4 and post-16. In the case of vocational courses, teachers need knowledge and experience of general vocational requirements, core skills, assessment methods and the relevant industrial, commercial or services sector.

Records of qualifications, experience and training, which include secure knowledge about the range and nature of pupils' particular special educational needs, provide a starting point. The main source of evidence is the observation of teaching, supported by study of teachers' planning and discussion with them.

Inspectors can judge teachers' subject knowledge by observing, for example, their:

◆ competence in teaching the content of the National Curriculum programmes of study and the RE syllabus, examination and vocational courses, or areas of learning;

◆ competence in planning activities and carrying them out;

◆ skill in asking relevant questions and providing explanations;

◆ perceptiveness in marking and responding to pupils' work;

◆ ability to draw on a range of contexts and resources to make subject knowledge comprehensible to pupils;

◆ success in providing demanding work for pupils of all abilities;

◆ skill in understanding how different pupils learn.

*Do teachers set high expectations so as to challenge pupils and deepen their knowledge and understanding?*

■ Inspectors need to identify the level of challenge in the content, activities and learning resources provided for pupils of different attainment. They should evaluate whether teaching is well matched to the pupils' stage of learning and moves them on.

Teachers' expectations of pupils relate closely to their knowledge of the subjects or areas of learning, their knowledge of what pupils have already achieved, and their understanding of how pupils will gain most from the teaching. Good teaching makes clear the importance of application, accuracy and good presentation, and the need to use critical thinking, creativity and imagination. It provides the stimulus, the knowledge and the methods for pupils to do their best in all these respects. Teaching should provide opportunities for students to take increasing responsibility for their own work.

Expectations may be set too low; they can also be pitched unrealistically high if pupils are not ready for the task or do not have adequate resources, support or time to undertake it effectively.

### Do teachers plan effectively?

■ Good planning means that the teaching in a lesson, session, or sequence of lessons has clear objectives for what pupils are to learn and how these objectives will be achieved. It will take into account the differing needs of pupils. Plans can take a number of forms; for example, schemes of work may include detailed lesson plans, but these may be separate. Whatever form planning takes, inspectors need to look for evidence of teaching intentions and how they will be met. They should look for evidence that planning:

   ◆ covers the areas of learning for under-fives;

   ◆ incorporates National Curriculum programmes of study, syllabus and course requirements and the requirements of the agreed syllabus for religious education, where appropriate;

   ◆ sets out clear objectives;

   ◆ summarises what pupils or students will do and the resources they will need;

   ◆ shows how knowledge and understanding can be extended and the work adapted to suit pupils and students who learn at different rates.

The teaching of younger children should be linked to the organisation of the classroom where planned activities are set up and resourced for teachers and children to select and use over longer periods of time. It should also provide for subject teaching sessions with groups, individual children and the whole class as deemed necessary to enable pupils to make progress.

Inspectors should pay particular attention to structure and progression in the planning of topics which involve a number of subjects. The planning should indicate very clearly the learning objectives and how teaching will be organised to challenge pupils, and evidence that continuity and progression in each subject has been considered.

Where possible, inspectors should also discuss with teachers the context of the session or lessons, how the lesson fits into a longer term plan and why, for example, particular methods are used. Such discussions provide insight into teachers' planning and their response to changing situations which are not always recorded on paper.

Inspectors will need to consider how support staff are used and how they are informed about teaching and learning objectives and involved in planning.

### Do teachers employ methods and organisational strategies which match curricular objectives and the needs of all pupils?

■ The choice of teaching methods and organisational strategies is a matter for the school and the teacher's discretion. This should be based upon the objectives of the lesson and factors such as the number of pupils, their age, attainment and behaviour, and the nature of the resources and accommodation.

## Guidance on using the schedule

The key to the judgement is whether the methods and organisation are fit for the purpose of achieving high standards of work and behaviour. Direct evidence will come from lesson observation. Scrutiny of pupils' work and discussion with teachers and pupils gives evidence over a longer timescale of whether methods and organisation are sufficiently responsive to the range of curricular objectives and pupils' needs.

Teaching methods include exposition, explanation, demonstration, discussion, practical activity, investigation, testing and problem-solving. The test of their effectiveness is the extent to which they extend or deepen pupils' knowledge and understanding and develop their skills. They are likely to do so when they are selected and handled with careful regard to:

◆ the nature of the curricular objectives being pursued; and

◆ what pupils know, understand and can do, and what they need to learn next.

This test applies to the range of methods – from sustained exposition to the use of practical work. In each case inspectors should consider, for example, whether:

◆ exposition or explanation by the teacher is informative, lively and well-structured;

◆ the teacher's use of questions probes pupils' knowledge and understanding and challenges their thinking;

◆ practical activity is purposeful in that pupils are encouraged to think about what they are doing, what they have learned from it and how to improve their work;

◆ investigations and problem-solving activities are efficient in helping pupils to apply and extend their learning in new contexts.

Key issues with regard to how pupils are organised in the class are:

◆ whether the objectives are best achieved by pupils working alone, in pairs or small groups, or all together;

◆ whether the form of organisation allows the teacher to interact with pupils positively and economically.

Good teaching will employ different organisational strategies to pursue different curricular objectives.

In relation to whole-class teaching inspectors should consider how well the teacher manages explanation, questioning and discussion so that all pupils are involved and stimulated. In observing group and individual work inspectors should look at how the teacher interacts with pupils to challenge their thinking and keep the work focused and moving at pace. Inspectors should identify whether the teacher is using his or her teaching skills rather than merely servicing the tasks. This is a particular issue when classroom activities cover a number of subjects and use a wide range of resources, including other adults.

In any form of organisation inspectors must consider the effectiveness of the strategies used for supporting pupils who may have a wide range of special educational needs and, where relevant, pupils for whom English is an additional language. In observing whole class or group work inspectors also need to be alert to how teachers make sure that all pupils participate and how they handle situations where individuals dominate or are passive.

*Do teachers manage pupils well and achieve high standards of discipline?*

*Do teachers use time and resources effectively?*

■ Central to the judgements relating to these criteria is the extent to which the management of time and resources contributes to pupils working productively – that is, spending a high proportion of the available time 'on task'.

A key point is whether the structuring and the pace of work help sustained learning to take place. In effective lessons or sessions the pace is usually brisk, but there are occasions when time for reflection and consolidation or for steady and careful pursuit of a task is required. In lessons, therefore, inspectors should judge whether:

◆ the structure of the lesson makes best use of the time available;

◆ pupils are clear about what they are doing, why they are doing it, how long they have to do it, and the way in which they can judge success in their work.

Taken together, these features are likely to motivate pupils and promote good behaviour.

Vocational courses in KS4 and post-16 put considerable emphasis on assignments. Teachers need to be aware of the impact that such tasks can have on pupils' other work and their management of time.

A judgement is needed about whether resources are appropriately chosen to advance pupils' learning. Resources include reference and other information materials; they may also include special equipment and support assistants. Some resources used may be outside the classroom – for example, reference material and IT equipment in a library or resource centre. Where possible, inspectors should evaluate the learning that occurs in these circumstances.

*Do teachers assess pupils' work thoroughly and constructively, and use assessments to inform teaching?*

■ Judgements about assessment should focus on how well the day-to-day interventions with pupils, including the marking of work, are used to help them understand what they need to do to improve their work and make progress.

Clues to the effectiveness of formative assessment are how well teachers listen and respond to pupils, encourage and where appropriate praise them, recognise and handle misconceptions, build on their responses and steer them towards new learning or clearer understanding. Interactions of this kind play an important part in the support and encouragement of pupils and may be seen in a variety of contexts including whole class lessons, group work and in individual tasks.

Scrutiny of pupils' books, and discussion with them, provide evidence of the quality of marking, how thoroughly problems are diagnosed, whether comments encourage and challenge and whether the approaches to marking are consistent throughout the school. It will be evident in written work whether feedback is having a positive effect.

Particular attention should be paid to how assessment of the work of pupils relates to targets set in individual education plans.

## Guidance on using the schedule

*Do teachers use homework effectively to reinforce and/or extend what is learnt in schools?*

■ Pupils of all ages may take work home, including reading books and mathematical work. For the under-fives, careful and judicious use of homework is important in providing a successful bridge from home to school and it can be influential in supporting and extending the curriculum throughout the primary years. Inspectors should establish whether the homework set is used and followed up in class and should evaluate the quality and relevance of what pupils are asked to do at home. As pupils progress through the school a carefully planned approach to homework can build up an individual pupil's capacity to work independently. This may vary according to pupils' needs and capabilities, but should be a part of many KS3, KS4 and post-16s' experiences. Evidence of the effectiveness of this approach should be seen, particularly in coursework assignments in KS4 and post-16. In certain residential special schools, time and a place for "homework" may need to be provided.

## MAIN SOURCES OF EVIDENCE

### Before the inspection

◆ the *Headteacher's Form* will give a preliminary view of staff experience, expertise, qualifications and training;

◆ the **staff handbook** (if available) may include a policy for teaching;

◆ **schemes of work and teachers' planning** documents should provide insights into the teaching methods and organisational strategies deployed in the school;

◆ the **assessment policy** should indicate how day-to-day formative assessment is intended to help provide pupils with appropriate and challenging work;

◆ **pre-inspection meetings** with the headteacher, governors and parents are likely to provide a range of perspectives on the overall quality of teaching at the school.

### During the inspection

◆ **observation of lessons** should focus on the effect of teaching on what pupils learn and on their attainment, progress and response;

◆ **statements of special educational need, annual reviews and individual education plans** provide evidence about teachers' planning to meet the particular needs of individual pupils. These may include programmes of work for implementation by support assistants or therapists;

◆ **a scrutiny of pupils' work** and how it is marked;

◆ **discussions with teachers, support staff, therapists and pupils** may provide insight into the extent to which the teaching sets high expectations and promotes the learning of all pupils.

**ADDITIONAL NOTES**

### TRAINEE TEACHERS

Where trainee teachers are taking a class during the inspection, the class should be inspected using the same criteria used to judge other teaching in the school. Section 9 inspections should not evaluate school-based elements of initial teacher training, but should comment on the school's participation in training teachers and in particular on the benefits to standards and quality in the school.

### SUPPLY TEACHERS

Teaching by supply teachers is part of the provision made by the school and should be inspected as such. Supply teachers will not necessarily have close knowledge of the pupils. The quality of the teaching they offer may be affected by the quality of the information they have been given about the work the class has been doing and should be doing and by whether they are expected to teach a one-off lesson, with or without materials provided. Where the incidence of supply teaching is significant, inspectors should note whether it has a bearing on the quality of provision and on pupils' attainment and progress.

**Inspection schedule**

## 5.2 THE CURRICULUM AND ASSESSMENT

**INSPECTORS MUST EVALUATE AND REPORT ON STRENGTHS AND WEAKNESSES IN**

■ the planning and content of the curriculum and its contribution to the educational standards achieved by all pupils, taking account of their age, attainment, gender, ethnicity, background and special educational need, including reference to:

i the areas of learning for children under 5, the subjects and courses provided from 5 to 16, and the post-16 curriculum;

ii the provision made for personal and social education, including health education, sex education where appropriate, and attention to drug misuse;

iii careers education and guidance in schools providing for the secondary age range;

iv extra-curricular activities, including sport;

■ procedures for assessing pupils' attainment.

*Judgements should be based on the extent to which the curriculum:*

◆ is balanced and broadly based, promotes pupils' intellectual, physical and personal development and prepares pupils for the next stage of education;

◆ meets statutory requirements to teach the subjects of the National Curriculum, religious education and sex education, where these apply;

◆ provides equality of access and opportunity for pupils to make progress;

◆ meets the curricular requirements of all pupils;

◆ is planned effectively, providing continuity and progression of learning;

◆ is enriched by extra-curricular provision, including sport;

◆ includes, for pupils of secondary age, careers education and impartial guidance, drawing on the careers service;

*and, in relation to assessment, the extent to which:*

◆ there are effective systems for assessing pupils' attainment;

◆ assessment information is used to inform curriculum planning.

## Guidance on using the schedule

### INSPECTION FOCUS

■ Inspection centres on the extent to which the content and organisation of the curriculum and its assessment provide access to the full range of learning experiences and promote the attainment, progress and personal development of all pupils. The curriculum comprises all the planned activities within and beyond the timetable.

■ The curriculum **for under-fives** should provide teaching in the following areas of learning[22]: language and literacy; mathematical; scientific and technological; human and social; aesthetic and creative; physical; moral and spiritual. The curriculum should take account of children's developing intellectual, physical, emotional and social abilities; make appropriate provision for purposeful play, talk and direct enquiry, together with opportunities for child-initiated activity. It should provide pupils with experiences that lead toward the National Curriculum programmes of study.

The curriculum of a **special school** complies with the 1988 Education Reform Act if it:

◆ is balanced and broadly based;

◆ promotes the spiritual, moral, cultural, mental and physical development of pupils;

◆ prepares pupils for the opportunities, responsibilities and experiences of adult life;

◆ includes the subjects of the National Curriculum as prescribed in regulations;

◆ provides for religious education in accordance with an agreed syllabus or the school's trust deeds;

◆ provides for sex education in accordance with the school's policy.

Schools should also provide careers education and guidance (for secondary age pupils), and health education, including education about drug misuse.

Planning, organisation and implementation of the curriculum should enable pupils in special schools to have full access to the curriculum to which all pupils are entitled. Individual entitlement to a broadly-based and balanced curriculum as set out in Section 1 of the 1988 Act cannot be modified or disapplied.

However, the curriculum, its management and organisation, whilst complying with statutory requirements, must also reflect the particular needs of individual pupils. Most special schools need to plan for a wide range of learning disabilities.

Schools will plan a curriculum which includes the programmes of study of the National Curriculum relevant to pupils' age and disabilities. This whole curriculum should be coherent and progressive.

Teaching developmentally relevant activities from the appropriate key stage programmes of study of the National Curriculum will normally occur, although schools may choose content from earlier key stages if it is necessary. A rationale for this planning decision should be provided.

---

22   Subject to any subsequent national guidance which may override this classification.

## Guidance on using the schedule

Pupils may be admitted to a special school at any time in the school year and numbers in key stages and year groups will fluctuate. This has significant implications for the planning of schemes of work.

Some pupils may remain on the roll of a special school from the age of two until they are 19. It is, therefore, essential that planning takes account of the need for progression in learning, continuity of experience, and age appropriateness, however small the learning steps.

The school's practice on assessment needs to be seen in relation to:

◆ records of progress for under-fives;

◆ the assessment requirements of the National Curriculum at the end of KS1, KS2 and KS3;

◆ public examination requirements at KS4 and post-16;

◆ the requirements covering pupil records and reports, including annual reports to parents and reports to school leavers;

◆ the additional requirements for the annual review of statements of special educational need.

Curriculum planning, organisational and resourcing arrangements for schools of different sizes and in different locations vary considerably. In some special schools curriculum planning often needs to take account of more than one year group and key stage within a class. Increasingly, in special schools the curriculum at KS3 and KS4 is organised into separate subjects taught by specialist teachers, but other forms of organisation may be used, for example in relation to vocational courses. Provision for curricular elements such as IT and health education may be organised in a variety of ways.

Some schools will be ensuring an opportunity at KS4 for pupils to exercise some choice over their curriculum and may feature different types of provision for different groups of pupils, as permitted by the Dearing review of the National Curriculum. The latter requires that students' competences are assessed in the workplace or through simulated activities and for this reason relatively few schools will offer them. The full GNVQ is normally part of post-16 provision; Part One GNVQs, taken from the full GNVQ, may be offered at KS4.[23] All courses require substantial records of students' work and internal and external verification of the standards of their work. A few special schools will offer A/AS-level courses.

When schools make provision for students post-16, a distinct curriculum with opportunities to link into the community and colleges of further education is required.

■ Overall judgements about the extent to which the curriculum meets the needs of all pupils should draw on the inspection of all the school's provision, with an emphasis on what is taught rather than what is documented. The latter will assume greater importance when little or no observation of teaching and learning in particular aspects of the curriculum is possible during the inspection.

---

23  Part One GNVQs are designed to occupy time equivalent to two GCSE subjects and to be broadly equivalent to the demands of GCSE. Pupils maintain a portfolio of work based on a vocational area and core skills in the application of number, communication and IT. At level 2, the core skills are deemed equivalent to GCSE grade C in English and Mathematics.

## Guidance on using the schedule

Where there is provision for pupils under five in reception classes, an evaluation is needed of how appropriate and balanced the curriculum is in relation to the areas of learning. In evaluating the curriculum for all key stages, inspectors should consider evidence about all the school's provision, including provision which meets National Curriculum and religious education requirements, the provision for personal and social education and for careers education and guidance (where appropriate), and the contribution of extra-curricular activities and external links.

When evaluating the post-16 curriculum inspectors should consider evidence of all the school's provision for its students.

Judgements are also required on the effectiveness of systems of assessment across the curriculum and the use of assessment for all curriculum planning to include individual education plans.

## USING THE CRITERIA

*Is the curriculum balanced and broadly based? Does it promote pupils' intellectual, physical and personal development and prepare pupils for the next stage of education?*

■ Inspectors need to establish whether the special school curriculum complies with Section 1 of the 1988 Education Reform Act. Although not subject to Section 1, the curriculum of nursery classes needs to be evaluated to see if it is balanced and broad, contributes to pupils' development and helps to prepare them for the National Curriculum.

Inspectors should take into account the review of the National Curriculum, which slimmed down what must be taught.

For 14-16 year olds, it is essential to consider the curriculum in the light of the Dearing Review, which resulted in:

◆ enhanced flexibility for schools by reducing the mandatory curriculum to a minimum core in English, mathematics and science; short courses in technology and a modern foreign language; physical education; religious education and sex education;

◆ schools being enabled to exploit this additional flexibility by making available other academic options and a wider range of vocational options designed to facilitate progression to vocational courses post-16.

The curriculum at KS4 should be judged in terms of the extent to which schools meet these national intentions.

Provision at KS4 and post-16 should ensure that individual pupils and students develop their understanding of adult life and are in a position to proceed to appropriate education, training or employment options. The school's provision should include sound and impartial careers education and guidance and involve parents where possible.

It is important that inspectors examine whether post-16 students are following courses which reflect their academic or vocational aspirations and their previous achievements, and have a good chance of achieving their objectives.

## Guidance on using the schedule

Discussions with pupils and students and analysis of a sample of individual timetables may be helpful in establishing how the curriculum works in practice. Inspectors should also consider the available information on the destinations of school leavers.

Documentation, including the school's curriculum policy, guidelines and schemes of work, is a starting point for evaluating whether the whole curriculum makes broad, balanced and coherent provision for all aspects of pupils' development.

*Does the curriculum meet statutory requirements to teach the subjects of the National Curriculum, religious education and sex education, where these apply?*

■ Provided statutory requirements are met, it is for the school to determine the character of its curriculum and the mode of its delivery. Judgements should be based on how well the organisation of the curriculum and assessment contribute to pupils' attainment, progress and response rather than on predetermined notions of what is desirable in curriculum organisation.

The National Curriculum can be taught as discrete subjects, in an integrated form (such as through topics, themes or modules) or as a combination of both. Whichever approach is adopted, planning and teaching need to pay due regard to the subject Orders. There should be clear evidence of programmes of study in classroom work observed. Adequate time needs to be made available for teaching the different components of the curriculum. The test is whether pupils are able to cover the required material in appropriate depth, in relation to their capabilities.

The governing body of a special school must have a policy on sex education (for pupils of primary age, provision is discretionary). Parents should be consulted and informed about the policy and any provision and should be informed about their rights to withdraw their children from some elements of any sex education programme. Sex education will often be found as part of a broader programme of health education. (Additional notes are given at the end of this section.)

*Does the curriculum provide equality of access and opportunity for pupils to learn and to make progress?*

■ Inspectors should consider how the curriculum planning and implementation take account of pupils' age and special educational need, gender, ethnicity and competence in English as an additional language, through the provision of appropriate teaching methods and materials. The curriculum should respond to the cultural heritage of pupils and promote equality of opportunity. Inspectors need to consider the impact of the organisation of pupils into class and teaching groups on ensuring equality of access and opportunity.

The National Curriculum programmes of study for each key stage should be taught to all pupils. For some pupils, material may be selected from earlier or later key stages to enable them to progress and demonstrate achievement, but this material should be in contexts suitable for pupils' ages.

Inspectors should evaluate how effectively time is used to provide for pupils' differing aptitudes, interests, aspirations and specific needs, and the suitability of the range and the accessibility to all pupils of any post-16 courses leading to qualifications (or other forms of accreditation).

*Does the curriculum meet the curricular requirements of all pupils on the school's Code of Practice special educational needs register?*

■ All pupils in a special school should be at stage 5 of the Code of Practice; a few may be awaiting assessment at stage 4. The whole curriculum of the school should meet the specific needs identified in learning objectives in individual education plans mainly within the programmes of study of the National Curriculum.

*Is the curriculum planned effectively, providing continuity and progression of learning?*

■ Inspectors should evaluate whether curriculum planning takes account of what has gone before and what will follow. The need for continuity and progression applies to the whole curriculum and to individual subjects and courses; it applies between years, between key stages and between schools and colleges. Evidence is needed of whether, as pupils move through the school, the curriculum builds systematically on existing knowledge, understanding and skills. In residential schools, evidence should be sought of curriculum links between the teaching and care staff.

The continuity and progression of the curriculum for the under-fives should give all children access to planned experiences and opportunities, both indoors and outdoors, that will form the foundations of learning at compulsory school age. Many of the activities planned should lead into the National Curriculum programmes of study.

Curriculum planning needs to make effective provision for the programmes of study, whatever type of organisation is adopted. Many schools use topic work as a major mode of curriculum organisation. Topics may be broad-based or have one subject as the major focus. If topics are broad-based, inspectors should evaluate how effectively they are planned to cater for the intended programmes of study and whether they provide a clear structure and sufficient progression.

A school may plan a two, three or four-year cycle for topics, often because classes contain two or more year groups. Where there is a wide age range, it is particularly important to check whether there is progression within the class, from one year to the next.

Planning is at its best where:

◆ there is whole school agreement about subject coverage and the balance between subjects and topics;

◆ outcomes are monitored by senior staff;

◆ there is consistency of work between classes; and

◆ reference is made not only to the knowledge, understanding and skills which teachers expect pupils to develop, but also to the teaching methods and organisational strategies to be employed to achieve these goals.

Inspectors should establish as far as they can the effectiveness of the school's systems for liaison with other schools and with further and higher education institutions and employers as pupils and students make the transition to other schools, further education, training or employment. Evidence is most likely to come from discussion with senior staff and teachers, and from study of a sample of pupils' records and work, but the issue may also feature in the parents' meeting.

## Guidance on using the schedule

*Is the curriculum enriched by extra-curricular provision, including sport?*

■ It is often difficult for special schools to arrange extra-curricular activities after school because of transport arrangements. Some schools run clubs and arrange visits to special events such as exhibitions and concerts. Sporting events are often organised within the school or on an area basis involving other schools. Inspectors should look for evidence of these being used to support, extend and enrich the curriculum, the extent of pupils' access, and the contribution made to their attainment, progress and personal development.

Where pupils are capable of participating, inspectors must inspect and report on the quality, time spent and range of games offered as part of the physical education curriculum and on the provision of sport outside formal lessons, paying particular attention to traditional team games. Reports should include pupil participation rates in extra-curricular sport, the number of teachers who supervise this activity, sports competitions within and between schools and any improvements the school has made in providing both curricular and extra-curricular competitive games.

*Does the curriculum include, for pupils of secondary age, careers education and impartial guidance, drawing on the careers service?*

■ Careers education should provide a planned programme to develop skills, knowledge and attitudes relating to choices and transitions to further education, training and employment. Careers guidance requires a systematic and personalised approach to helping pupils make choices appropriate to them through impartial advice. Both elements, careers education and guidance, should be part of a wider approach to preparing pupils for adult life.

The school's documentation should show how careers education is co-ordinated, how it draws on pupils' experience within subjects and is enhanced by links with employers and training providers, for example through work experience. Inspectors need to look for evidence that work experience is well planned, effectively monitored and followed up. The effectiveness of the school's links with employers in this and other ways should be reported in Section 5.5.

In relation to careers guidance, inspectors need to judge how effectively the school provides impartial and well-informed advice, drawing on the expertise of outside agencies, particularly the careers service, and relates to the pupils' and students' disabilities. The school's liaison with the careers service should be based on a clear specification of what each party will arrange and provide. Inspectors need to check that the information available to pupils relating to further and higher education, training and employment is up to date, accessible, comprehensive and appropriate for the range of pupils in the school.

Inspectors need to judge whether careers education and guidance is objective and even-handed. It must also be free from gender or other stereotyping – for example, in encouraging girls as well as boys towards careers in science and engineering.

Consideration should be given to whether those involved in providing careers education and guidance have access to appropriate professional development to prepare and assist them in their work. Professional development is covered in Section 6.2.

*Are there effective systems for assessing pupils' attainment?*

*Is assessment information used to inform curriculum planning?*

■ Inspectors should evaluate whether assessments are accurate and used to plan future work to help pupils make progress. They need to establish whether teachers' assessments relate accurately to National Curriculum requirements, and external validation arrangements where these apply.

A review of documentation and discussion with teachers and staff responsible for co-ordination and liaison provides a context for the assessment observed in lessons. Inspectors need to establish whether the teachers' assessments relate accurately to the National Curriculum requirements where these apply. Evidence includes comparison of pupils' work with teachers' assessments and records. Particular attention needs to be given to the use of assessment in planning a response to the needs and range of individual pupils. Annually updated pupil records, annual reviews and transition planning need to conform to statutory requirements. They also have a key role in ensuring that information on pupils' performance is transferred and used as they move through the school and from one stage of education to the next.

The appropriateness of accreditation at KS4 and post-16 to meet individual needs and provide opportunity for progression should be examined. In vocational courses in both KS4 and post-16, assessment may involve teachers working closely with people in industry, commerce or services.

Pupil records have a key role in ensuring that information on pupils' performance is transferred and used as they move through the school and from one stage of education to the next. Schools must keep formal educational records on every pupil, including material on academic achievements, other skills and abilities and progress in school, and must update these records at least once a year. Parents of pupils of compulsory school age must be given access to these records and they must be transferred if the pupil moves to another school. A variety of procedures apply locally to the transfer of information between schools, although all are underpinned by the requirement to pass on pupils' educational records. Particular features of liaison to encourage continuity and progression in learning may include feedback on the progress of former pupils, and opportunities for staff and pupils to work alongside one another on joint activities.

## Guidance on using the schedule

### MAIN SOURCES OF EVIDENCE

#### Before the inspection

◆ the *Headteacher's Form* and school prospectus should show, at least in outline, how far the school's planned curriculum meets statutory requirements;

◆ curriculum policies, guidelines or schemes of work will provide an indication of the extent to which the planned curriculum meets the various inspection criteria;

◆ school curriculum audits or analyses (if available) may offer useful insights;

◆ discussion at pre-inspection meetings with the headteacher, governors and parents is likely to provide a range of perspectives on the curriculum;

◆ information supplied by the local TEC (Training and Enterprise Council) through the school may contain significant evidence about course provision, links with business, careers education and guidance, and details of locally agreed targets.

#### During the inspection

A comparison of curriculum plans and practice will be obtained from:

◆ observations of lessons, including shadowing individual pupils' experience of the curriculum;

◆ observation of the 24-hour curriculum for boarding pupils, where relevant;

◆ analysis and observation of extra-curricular activities for all pupils;

◆ a scrutiny of samples of pupils' work and records, including records of NC assessments;

◆ discussions with teachers, support staff, other involved professionals and pupils, concentrating on how curriculum organisation affects pupils' attainment and progress;

◆ an examination of individual education plans, statements and annual reviews to establish the appropriateness of provision for individual pupils.

**ADDITIONAL NOTES**

## HEALTH EDUCATION

Health education should play a role in promoting the physical, social and emotional well-being of pupils. Aspects of health education are found in subjects (for example, within the programmes of study for science) and in the daily routines of the school. Provision may also make an important contribution to pupils' personal development including moral, social and cultural aspects. Inspectors will need to establish: whether provision is planned, coherent, and appropriate to the ages and needs of pupils, and whether pupils have a sound knowledge and understanding of health issues, and an awareness of their ability to make choices relating to their health. Sex education may be an element of health education provision. School staff and other providers need to be well briefed and sensitive to the agreed approach to health education in the school and to the ages and needs of pupils.

## DRUGS EDUCATION

The National Curriculum Science Order states the statutory minimum that pupils should be taught about drugs. Schools are free to decide for themselves how best to organise drug education for their pupils. They may provide it within science lessons, as appropriate within other subject areas, or as part of a broader programme of personal and social or health education. The essential aim of drug education should be to give pupils the facts, emphasise the benefits of a healthy lifestyle, and give young people the knowledge and skills to make informed and healthy choices now and later in life.

Inspectors should also determine whether schools have clear policies and procedures for dealing with drug-related incidents on the school premises and for working with other services concerned with young people to offer appropriate support and advice. DFEE Circular 4/95 offers guidance on drug education and the management of drug-related incidents.

## GENERAL NATIONAL VOCATIONAL QUALIFICATIONS (GNVQS)

GNVQs are broad-based vocational qualifications which cover a wide range of occupational areas and provide opportunities to prepare pupils for further and higher education and employment. The awards are designed primarily for full-time students between the ages of 16 and 19. Part One GNVQs, taken from the full GNVQ, may be offered at KS4 and are designed to occupy time equivalent to two GCSE subjects and to be broadly equivalent to the demands of GCSE. Relatively few schools offer NVQs because of the requirement to assess competencies in the workplace or through simulated activities.

## Guidance on using the schedule

GNVQs are available at three levels: **Advanced** GNVQ, or 'vocational A-Level', is equivalent to at least two GCE A-levels, NVQ level 3 or BTEC National Certificates/Diplomas; **Intermediate** GNVQ is equivalent to four or five GCSEs at grades A to C, NVQ level 2, or BTEC First Certificates/Diplomas; **Foundation** GNVQ is equivalent to four GCSEs graded D-G or NVQ level 1.

Each GNVQ is made up of four types of unit:

◆ mandatory vocational units covering the skills, knowledge and understanding needed for a broad range of jobs;

◆ mandatory core skills units, which further develop skills in communication, application of number and IT. The core skills units are outlined at five levels of attainment and these have been broadly linked with the National Curriculum. Students can be encouraged to work to levels of attainment in core skills units at levels above their main award;

◆ optional vocational units, which give students an opportunity to specialise;

◆ additional units, which allow for further study, for example, Personal skills – working with others; Personal skills – improving own learning and performance; Problem-solving.

Each unit is expressed in the form of elements (which describe the activity to be assessed); performance criteria (which provide a means of judging successful performance of the activity), range statements (which describe the range of settings in which the activity should be performed successfully) and evidence indicators (which describe the type and sufficiency of evidence that should be presented for assessment). These, together with the compulsory requirement for a pass in an end-of-unit test, are the means of setting the national standard. Tasks and assignments are assessed against the standards. Work assessed as a pass can be further graded according to additional criteria for the award of merit or distinction. Inspectors will need to determine whether there are appropriate systems for assessment and recording and for internal verification to check the standard of pupils' work.

The GNVQ framework enables a flexible approach to delivery. The outcomes of various activities – for example, assignments, projects, work experience, group discussion – are collected in a portfolio which is used as evidence for assessment. Because these courses are based on assessment in relation to outcomes, it is not possible to rely only on classroom observation as a means of judging standards of attainment. Inspectors will need to talk with students and scrutinise completed work in order to evaluate what pupils know, understand and can do in the vocational area and in the core skills. Inspectors will need to evaluate whether the completed work meets the GNVQ criteria and whether it is at an appropriate level of knowledge, understanding and intellectual skills for the level of the course and its stated equivalence (GCSE or GCE A-level).

The components of the course should be well co-ordinated and provision coherent. Vocational units should be staffed by teachers who have a good knowledge and understanding of the vocational and occupational areas and the contribution of these to further stages of education, training and employment. The core skills element of courses should be appropriately designed or taught by teachers experienced in English, mathematics and IT teaching. GNVQ courses should, where appropriate, include fieldwork, visits and simulations. These elements frequently require that the school has established appropriate links with local industry, commerce and the community.

## 5.3 PUPILS' SPIRITUAL, MORAL, SOCIAL AND CULTURAL DEVELOPMENT

### INSPECTORS MUST EVALUATE AND REPORT ON

■ the strengths and weaknesses of the school's provision for the spiritual, moral, social and cultural development of all pupils, through the curriculum and life of the school, the example set for pupils by adults in the school; and the quality of the act of collective worship[24].

*Judgements should be based on the extent to which the school:*

◆ provides its pupils with knowledge and insight into values and beliefs and enables them to reflect on their experiences in a way which develops their spiritual awareness and self-knowledge;

◆ teaches the principles which distinguish right from wrong;

◆ encourages pupils to relate positively to others, take responsibility, participate fully in the community, and develop an understanding of citizenship;

◆ teaches pupils to appreciate their own cultural traditions and the diversity and richness of other cultures.

---

[24] The report should state, in Section 6.1, the school's compliance with statutory requirements, where these apply.

## Guidance on using the schedule

### INSPECTION FOCUS

■ Evaluation of provision for pupils' spiritual, moral, social and cultural development links four aspects of personal development in which schools have an important part to play. In this section inspectors need to evaluate what schools actively do to *promote* pupils' development. Although each aspect of spiritual, moral, social and cultural development can be viewed separately, provision is likely to be interconnected and evaluation should reflect this.

There is a strong link with Sections 4.2, 5.1 and 5.2: the curriculum and its teaching provide the major vehicle for promoting personal development in all its forms. A major part is also played by the relationships that are established in a school and the support and guidance provided for pupils, covered in Section 5.4, and the partnership with parents and the community, covered in Section 5.5.

■ The responsibility of the class teacher for all or most of the curriculum in special schools facilitates a coherent approach to pupils' spiritual, moral, social and cultural development and their intellectual development. The approach should be informed by links with parents and supported by the sense of a close community which is often developed in nursery and primary schools.

Inspectors should evaluate the extent to which provision reaches all pupils whatever their background. Some pupils may need additional support and encouragement to take a full part in school activities and to accept and exercise responsibilities.

■ Overall judgements are concerned with the opportunities given for pupils to learn about and explore different values, beliefs and views and to develop and express their own. Judgements should be based on evidence from the whole curriculum and the day-to-day life of the school, including the examples set by adults and the quality of collective worship. This is an area on which evidence must be drawn from all members of the team before considered corporate judgements are made. The judgements are best made in conjunction with those on other aspects of provision.

### USING THE CRITERIA

*Does the school provide its pupils with knowledge and insight into values and religious beliefs and enable them to reflect on their experiences in a way which develops their self-knowledge and spiritual awareness?*

■ Effective provision for spiritual development at the nursery and primary stage depends on a curriculum and approaches to teaching which embody clear values and enable pupils to gain understanding through reflection on their own and other people's lives and beliefs, and their environment. It relies on teachers receiving and valuing pupils' ideas across the whole curriculum, for example, in stories, in pupils' writing, art, music, history and in religious education. Acts of collective worship play a particular part. To the extent that spiritual insights imply an awareness of how pupils relate to others, there is a strong link to both moral and social development. All these components will manifest themselves in both the educational and care environment of residential schools.

## Guidance on using the schedule

Although religious education and spiritual development are not seen as synonymous, religious education can make a significant contribution to spiritual development. Inspectors might consider, for example, whether religious education encourages pupils to consider life's fundamental questions and how religious teaching can relate to them; respond to such questions with reference to the teachings and practices of religions as well as from their own experience and viewpoint; and reflect on their own beliefs or values in the light of what they are studying in religious education.

Inspection of acts of collective worship is needed in special schools which do not provide denominational education. Evaluation should focus on whether acts of worship are well planned and encourage pupils to explore questions about meaning and purpose, values and beliefs. Compliance with statutory requirements on collective worship should be reported in Section 6.1. (Guidance on the inspection of collective worship is given at the end of this section.)

### Does the school teach the principles which separate right from wrong?

■ The essence of moral development is to build a framework of values which regulate personal behaviour through principles rather than through fear of punishment or reward. Pupils are able to make moral decisions through the application of reason, even though they may not cope quite so securely with problems in which they are emotionally involved: in other words, their learning about moral issues may be on a different plane from their behaviour. Moral and social education are closely related and depend on the school fostering values such as honesty, fairness and respect for truth and justice.

Inspectors should consider whether the school provides a moral code as a basis for behaviour which is promoted through the life of the school. They should also look at the opportunities for pupils to develop and express moral values and extend social and personal understanding across a range of issues, including, for example, personal rights and responsibilities and equal opportunities. In all areas of the curriculum pupils can be encouraged to explore ideas about such issues. Well-chosen stories, the moral and social issues raised through the study of warfare, the interaction of people, resources and the environment, and the ways in which science and technology can affect our lives, are further examples. Sensitive discussion of incidents that arise in school or outside it may be also used to help children distinguish right from wrong behaviour.

### Does the school encourage pupils to relate effectively to others, take responsibility, participate fully in the community and develop an understanding of citizenship?

■ Social development hinges on an acceptance of group rules and the ability to set oneself in a wider context. Young children and adolescents may find that the need to be socially compliant is sometimes at odds with their developing moral sensibility. Partly for this reason, the quality of relationships in special schools is of crucial importance in forming the children's attitudes to co-operation, good social behaviour and self-discipline; for many children in special schools this social development is a central aim of their education.

Inspectors need to consider how the school, through its organisation, curriculum and other activities, contributes to social development through experience and understanding of social relationships and the rights and responsibilities of individuals within the social setting. Evidence may include opportunities for pupils to work co-operatively in lessons on projects or in games involving competition, discipline and fair play. Account should be taken of opportunities for pupils to take responsibility, demonstrate initiative and contribute to the life of the school as a community. Vocational courses at KS4 and post-16 can play a significant part in their development.

**Guidance on using the schedule**

*Does the school teach pupils to appreciate and develop their own cultural traditions and appreciate the diversity and richness of other cultures?*

■ Cultural development is concerned both with participation in and appreciation of cultural traditions.

The school's approach should be active. Inspectors need to look for evidence of how the school seeks to enrich its pupils' knowledge and experience of their own and other cultural traditions, through the curriculum and through visits, clubs and other activities. Aspects of the curriculum such as history, geography, art, music, dance, drama, and literature can all make positive contributions, for example, through opportunities for pupils to:

◆ visit museums and art galleries;

◆ work with artists, authors and performers;

◆ develop openness towards and value the music and dance of different cultures;

◆ appreciate the natural world through art and literature;

◆ recognise the contribution of many cultures to mathematics and to scientific and technological development.

## Guidance on using the schedule

## MAIN SOURCES OF EVIDENCE

**Before the inspection**

◆ **analysis of the school prospectus, curricular documentation, staff handbook and code of behaviour** should give a preliminary view of how the school seeks to promote pupils' spiritual, moral, social and cultural development;

◆ **discussion with governors and the headteacher** should be used to explore these preliminary views;

◆ **discussion with parents** at the pre-inspection meeting and analysis of the returns from the questionnaire may produce further evidence.

**During the inspection**

Evidence of the quality, range and impact of provision can be found through:

◆ **observation of lessons and the daily routines** in and around the school and in the residential setting, where appropriate; collective worship and assemblies, extra-curricular activities;

◆ **scrutiny of records of residential and other visits;**

◆ **examination of the syllabus for religious education, curriculum guidelines and schemes of work;**

◆ **assessment of the range and quality of resources** used to bring pupils into contact with different aspects of social and cultural traditions;

◆ **observations of pupils' responsibilities** around the school and opportunities for pupils' own initiatives;

◆ **discussions** with pupils, teachers and other adults, on the moral values promoted by the school;

◆ **observation** to establish whether pupils are treated consistently.

**ADDITIONAL NOTES**

## COLLECTIVE WORSHIP

The law requires special schools to secure that, so far as is practicable, every pupil attending the school will attend daily collective worship and receive religious education. Taken over a term, the majority of such acts of worship should be wholly or mainly of a broadly Christian character. The school prospectus should make clear parents' right to withdraw their children from collective worship. Defining worship is difficult because a wide variety of activities is used by people of all faiths. In forming a judgement about the character and quality of worship in schools, the following points may be helpful:

◆ worship is generally understood to imply the recognition of a supreme being. It should be clear that the words used and/or the activities observed in worship recognise the existence of a deity;

◆ much that is identifiably Christian in tone, may not necessarily mention Jesus. This is true of some hymns and prayers used regularly as part of worship within Christian churches. However, if the worship consistently avoids reference to Jesus within the spoken or written word then it could not reasonably be defined as mainly Christian;

◆ collective worship should not be judged by the presence or absence of a particular ingredient. It might include: sharing values of a Christian nature; opportunities for prayers or meditation; opportunities to reflect upon readings from holy texts or other writings which bring out religious themes; performance of music, drama and/or dance;

◆ each act of worship in a school should be considered as a piece. Before reaching a judgement the activities observed during the inspection should be set alongside the evidence of what has occurred, and is planned, over a term. If on balance it is judged that what the school provides is not in keeping with the spirit of the law, then this should be recorded and the reason(s) given. (Section 6.1 covers non-compliance with statutory requirements);

◆ worship may be judged not to fulfil statutory requirements but could still be observed to make a powerful contribution to spiritual, moral, social and cultural development. That should be made clear in the report.

## 5.4 SUPPORT, GUIDANCE AND PUPILS' WELFARE[25]

### INSPECTORS MUST EVALUATE AND REPORT ON

■ strengths and weaknesses in the school's provision for the educational and personal support and guidance of pupils and its contribution to educational standards achieved, taking account of individual needs, and the steps taken to ensure pupils' welfare;

■ the school's arrangements for child protection;

■ any matters which, in the view of inspectors, constitute a threat to health and safety.

*Judgements should be based on the extent to which the school:*

◆ provides effective support and advice for all its pupils, informed by monitoring of their academic progress, personal development, behaviour and attendance;

◆ has effective measures to promote discipline and good behaviour and eliminate oppressive behaviour including all forms of harassment and bullying;

◆ has effective child protection procedures;

◆ is successful in promoting the health, safety and general well-being of its pupils.

---

[25] Where boarding provision is included in the contract, evaluation of its quality should be included in this section of the report.

**Guidance on using the schedule**

## INSPECTION FOCUS

■ The school's support and guidance should enable all pupils to take full advantage of the educational opportunities offered and to have high but realistic expectations of themselves. The inspection should focus on the extent to which these ends are achieved through monitoring of progress and personal development, through individual support and advice, and through a climate in which pupils' well-being is paramount.

■ Support and guidance are provided largely by the class teacher or by a personal tutor at secondary level. They occur through the informal relationships which pervade the school, the planned curriculum and the consistent implementation of clear policies. Opportunities for informal support occur during the daily routines such as registration, meal times, play and story times. In some special schools, guidance is given in relation to personal and social education through a special programme of teaching.

For pupils entering school for the first time it may be their first prolonged separation from home. The way in which they are supported and helped as well as the arrangements for their welfare and security should be assessed. This is particularly important in residential schools.

Essential to the effectiveness of any school are the ways in which they promote regular attendance, good behaviour and respect for others. Action to prevent and deal with harassment and bullying are normally part of the school's behaviour and discipline policy and may feature in teaching programmes.

Schools will normally have regular contacts with other agencies, such as police, health, psychological and social services. In relation to child protection, schools have responsibility for reporting to, and liaising with, other agencies on the progress of children placed on the child protection register.

■ Overall judgements about support, guidance and welfare need to draw on the evidence of the whole team from all aspects of the school's work.

Information obtained in discussions with staff, pupils, parents/carers, visiting specialists and, where appropriate the independent listener, should be assessed against documents, policies, statements and written procedures about statutory requirements.

Inspectors will need to determine, overall, whether the school has done all that it can to support, guide and safeguard the welfare and well-being of all pupils including those whose advocacy skills are in the early stages of development. This should enable inspectors to judge the effectiveness of procedures and practices on educational standards achieved.

Any matters which in the view of the inspectors constitute a serious threat to the health and safety of staff and visitors as well as pupils must be reported in this section and in the **key issues for action**. Where there is a breach of statutory requirements, this should be reported in Section 6.1.

## Guidance on using the schedule

## USING THE CRITERIA

*Does the school provide effective support, advice and guidance for all its pupils, informed by monitoring of their academic progress, personal development, behaviour and attendance?*

■ Inspectors should assess how well staff interact with pupils within and outside the classroom, their accessibility and responsiveness to pupils' needs, and the quality of the support they give. The key is the impact on pupils' progress, general confidence and ability to cope effectively with everyday life in the school. Particular attention should be paid to how pupils are helped to meet the objectives in their individual education plans. Inspectors need to assess as far as is practicable the quality of liaison with support agencies and their impact on support for pupils. It may be possible to discuss this with visiting staff.

In relation to attendance, inspectors should establish whether the requirements for recording and reporting attendance are met, how the school follows up any unauthorised absence and any ways in which it monitors and seeks to improve attendance, in conjunction, for example, with the LEA. They should also consider, where appropriate, the support given to pupils who have had a prolonged period of absence.

*Does the school have effective measures to promote discipline and good behaviour and eliminate oppressive behaviour including all forms of harassment and bullying?*

■ While evidence of the school's intentions can be gained from documents on policy and procedures, the emphasis should be on the consistency of practice. Evaluation against the criterion should link with Section 4.2. Attention should be given to how the school creates a climate for good behaviour, as well as how it deals with specific incidents of misbehaviour. During the inspection, observation, discussion with staff and with pupils and analysis of the use of records will provide the basis for judgements. It is important to evaluate how effectively all staff promote the good behaviour of pupils through the school and residential setting.

In relation to harassment and bullying, inspectors need to assess how well the school recognises and records incidents that occur, how well it deals with them and what steps are taken to prevent repetition. It will be important to evaluate how consistently staff deal with such incidents across the 24-hour curriculum.

*Does the school have effective child protection procedures?*

■ Inspectors should evaluate whether the school is in a position to comply with local child protection procedures and whether the school's approach helps pupils to protect themselves and understand the importance of protecting others. A particular focus is how the school deals with instances of possible child abuse and its procedures for liaison with other agencies where children are on the child protection register. Inspectors should establish whether staff are aware of the procedures and how they raise pupils' awareness of child protection issues.

Where the registered inspector has reasonable grounds to believe that specific instances of possible child abuse are not being dealt with satisfactorily by the school, the relevant authority, normally the social services child protection team, should be contacted.

Additional notes on child protection are given at the end of this section.

*Is the school successful in promoting the health, safety and general well-being of its pupils?*

■ Inspectors should judge whether the school does all it reasonably can to protect the pupils in its charge from harm, and promotes their well-being through awareness of health and safety and through its day-to-day procedures. Evidence will come from examination of documents, from discussion and from observation of day-to-day procedures, such as those covering the organisation of school meals, the care of property, and the arrangements for and the conduct of visits. Attention should be given to first-aid and other medical support given by the school, including arrangements for pupils with specific physical or medical needs. Inspectors should be alert to features of the premises, equipment or working practices of the school which may impact on pupils' well-being.

Inspectors should ensure that the requirements to arrange periodic medical and dental inspections are fulfilled and that suitable arrangements are made to maintain the confidentiality of records. It is important to evaluate the safety and suitability of accommodation, both school and residential provision, to ensure its appropriateness for the age, ability and needs of the pupils, including a right to privacy. In residential schools it is important to ensure that an independent listener is available and accessible to all pupils; that the attention given to night-time cover and supervision is appropriate. Inspectors should also consider the effectiveness of the pupils' complaints procedures and their accessibility and relevance to their needs. Inspectors should assess whether the use of restraint (where used) is justified, appropriately documented and reflects the school's policy.

Additional notes on health and safety are given at the end of this section.

## Guidance on using the schedule

## MAIN SOURCES OF EVIDENCE

### Before the inspection

◆ the **pre-inspection meeting** with parents provides important evidence on the provision and effectiveness of pupils' support and guidance. Discussions may include how well pupils are known by staff, are helped to feel secure, the extent of support, guidance and encouragement, particularly in times of difficulty, and how effectively the school deals with poor behaviour and any instances of bullying;

◆ the **school prospectus**, and other information to parents;

◆ **school documentation** relating to policies and procedures on behaviour and discipline, bullying, pupils' welfare, health and safety and child protection; equal opportunities and special educational needs policies.

### During the inspection

Particular attention needs to be paid to:

◆ **observation and discussion with pupils** to establish whether policy and practice correspond and if there is consistency across the school;

◆ **procedures** for dealing with harassment, bullying and child protection and whether these are understood by all staff;

◆ **scrutiny** of records of incidents of oppressive behaviour;

◆ **an examination of individual education plans, statements and annual reviews;**

◆ **scrutiny** of care plans under the Children Act 1989, where applicable;

◆ **procedures** for supporting pupils absent for long periods;

◆ **discussion** with governors, staff and pupils will establish whether policy and practice correspond;

◆ **discussion** with the education welfare officer and visiting staff from other agencies where practical;

◆ **observation** of arrangements for pupils' safe arrival and departure from school;

◆ **discussion** with staff who link with social services and pupils being 'looked after';

◆ **inspection** of the effectiveness of the role and function of residential care officers, where appropriate, and relationships with teachers;

◆ **health and safety issues**, in relation to the accommodation and site, learning resources, school routines and practices, and visits.

**ADDITIONAL NOTES**

## CHILD PROTECTION

Schools play an important part in protecting children and a high proportion of children at risk are referred by teachers. All schools need to be vigilant because the incidence of sexual and emotional abuse is not related to social and economic circumstances.

DES Circular 4/88 gave guidance on child protection procedures within the education service. This circular was part of an inter-agency approach which was subsequently revised by the Children Act 1989. Further inter-agency guidance can be found in *Working Together under the Children Act 1989: a guide to arrangements for inter-agency co-operation for the protection of children from abuse*. Inspectors should establish that schools comply with this guidance by:

◆ designating a senior member of staff to have responsibility under procedures established by the Area Child Protection Committee (ACPC) and the LEA for co-ordinating action within the school and liaison with other agencies;

◆ following local ACPC procedures and promptly referring suspected cases of child abuse to the local social services department, or to the police, which are the investigative agencies in case of child protection;

◆ liaising with all other agencies involved in the protection of children, by monitoring the progress of children placed on the child protection register, by submitting reports to social services departments and case conferences, and by being represented at child protection case conferences;

◆ contributing to the prevention of child abuse through teaching which builds awareness of the dangers of abuse, helps children to protect themselves and develops responsible attitudes to adult life and parenthood;

◆ taking part in training which leads to a greater understanding of the signs and symptoms of child abuse, familiarises participants with ACPC and LEA procedures for dealing with individual cases, informs them about the roles and responsibilities of the other agencies with whom the school has to liaise, and gives advice on making use of the curriculum to build preventive approaches to child protection.

## HEALTH AND SAFETY

Controlling health and safety risks is an essential part of educational provision. The emphasis in the inspection should be on the extent to which the school responds to statutory requirements to establish, monitor and review the effectiveness of safe working procedures. Inspectors are not expected to carry out an audit of health and safety practice, but to report on what they see.

## Guidance on using the schedule

The registered inspector will need to:

◆ check that the school is aware of the need to comply with statutory requirements for health and safety and has a clear written policy and procedures to identify and control health and safety risks;

◆ judge whether the school has a responsible attitude towards the education and training of pupils in safety procedures;

◆ record any health and safety irregularities observed during the inspection and bring these to the attention of the headteacher and, where potentially serious, the employer;

◆ alert the Health and Safety Executive where there is an imminent risk of serious injury and the employer appears likely to refuse to remedy the situation as a matter of urgency;

◆ record serious matters in the inspection report, in the **key issues for action.**

**Before the inspection** the registered inspector should establish through the *Headteacher's Statement* that the school has a policy and procedures to identify, control, record and report health and safety risks. Important features are:

◆ a written statement of health and safety policy;

◆ the designation of one or more members of staff responsible for the implementation of policy;

◆ procedures for monitoring and reporting;

◆ arrangements for dealing with accidents and emergencies;

◆ details of health and safety training of staff with particular responsibilities, such as first-aid, the use of specified materials and equipment, the supervision of outdoor activities;

◆ a record of any identified health and safety concerns and the action taken or proposed.

**During the inspection** inspectors should judge the extent to which the policy and procedures are known and put into practice. Inspectors will need to take account of health and safety when evaluating pupils' behaviour, the accommodation and site, the learning resources, the teaching and the provision of educational activities, including visits. They should, for example, be alert to evidence of:

◆ safe practice in play areas, classrooms and specialist areas;

◆ attention to health and safety in the preparation and conduct of visits out of school;

◆ pupils' knowledge of safe working procedures;

◆ provision of a safe environment with due attention to the layout, placement of equipment and materials, the condition of floors and play areas;

◆ equipment which is well maintained and in safe condition;

◆ general cleanliness of floors and surfaces;

◆ appropriate arrangements for the provision, storage, administration and recording of first-aid equipment and medication;

◆ clean and suitable arrangements for the consumption of food.

## Guidance on using the schedule

Subject inspectors will need to establish that safe procedures are followed in their respective fields[26]. These include, for example, whether pupils are using eye or face shields in science and technology during practical work; whether machines and equipment are in safe positions in workshops; whether kilns are guarded to prevent pupils from touching hot surfaces; and whether flammable and corrosive substances are correctly stored.

---

[26]  For guidance on health and safety issues in subjects of the curriculum, useful references are:
*Safety in Science Education*, DFEE 1995; *Managing Health and Safety in School Workshops*, National Association of Advisers and Inspectors of Design and Technology (NAAIDT); *Managing Health and Safety in Food and Textiles*, National Association of Advisors and Inspectors of Design and Technology (NAAIDT); *Health and Safety in Workshops*, BS4163 ; *Safe Practice in Physical Education*, British Association of Advisers and Lecturers in PE (BAALPE).

**Inspection schedule**

## 5.5 PARTNERSHIP WITH PARENTS AND THE COMMUNITY

### INSPECTORS MUST EVALUATE AND REPORT ON

■ the effectiveness of the school's partnership with parents, highlighting strengths and weaknesses, in terms of:

i   the information provided about the school and about pupils' work and progress through annual and other reports and parents' meetings;

ii  parents' involvement with the school and with their children's work at home;

■ the contribution which the school's links with the community make to pupils' attainment and personal development.

*Judgements should be based on the extent to which:*

◆ links with parents contribute to pupils' learning;

◆ the school's work is enriched by links with the community, including employers, and provision for work experience for pupils of secondary age;

◆ the school promotes pupils' contributions to the local community, including through voluntary service in secondary schools.

**Guidance on using the schedule**

## INSPECTION FOCUS

- A close partnership between school and parents[27] can support pupils' progress. The focus of inspection should be on the extent to which parents support the work of the school and are informed about their children's progress. Similarly, inspectors should look at the way in which the school involves the local community and how this affects pupils' attainment, progress and personal development.

- Schools should encourage a partnership with parents to support their children's learning. In many schools, staff make home visits to children and parents before children enter school. Often schools actively promote the partnership by having parents work with them in the classrooms and help with school visits, by sending books or work home and by having regular meetings and activities.

  Where pupils board and are placed by authorities some distance from the school the most important feature of a home-school partnership is the quality of the contact. Regular meetings between the home and the school may not be possible and parents' ability to assist in educational visits or in the classroom is limited by virtue of the distance between the home and the school. In these circumstances the school will do all that it reasonably can to inform parents of their child's progress; to encourage active participation in matters important to the well-being of the child, for example attendance at annual reviews; and to encourage parents to participate at a distance in the life of the school through, for example, newsletters, photographs, or copies of work that illustrate effort and achievement. In some residential schools particular arrangements are made to transport parents from certain locations to the school for attendance at reviews and at school functions and, in addition, some schools provide accommodation for parents on-site for limited periods of time.

  Contact between school and home is usually the responsibility of the class teacher, although the nature of contact and the extent to which parents are involved in knowing what their children are doing, how they are getting on and how to help them, will be a matter of school policy.

  The arrangements for reporting to parents vary but are based on the statutory requirement to give parents regular information about pupils' attainment and opportunities to discuss their child's progress. All pupils will have a regular review and at least an annual review, involving parents as well as support agencies.

  Many schools have close links with the local community, and Training and Enterprise Councils (TECs), local industry, commerce and services. Some are used directly to enrich the curriculum provision; others, such as involvement with charities and local organisations, contribute to pupils' personal development.

- Overall judgements need to establish whether:

  - there are clear lines of communication;
  - the school's approach to relations with parents is maintained consistently;
  - the school does all it can to gain the involvement of all parents.

---

[27] The use of the word parent is synonymous with guardian/carer throughout this guidance.

## Guidance on using the schedule

In relation to links with the community, judgements need to draw on the range of activities and their impact on pupils' attainment, progress and personal development.

## USING THE CRITERIA

*Do links with parents contribute to pupils' learning?*

- Evaluation should focus on the extent to which the school involves parents as partners in their children's learning. Evidence of parental involvement will derive from discussion and direct observation and from assessing the quality of information provided for parents, including the prospectus. Inspectors should evaluate how the school communicates information to parents for whom English is an additional language.

Inspectors should explore how well the school helps parents to understand the curriculum, the teaching it provides, and how this can lead to teachers and parents working together to provide support at home, for example through paired reading. Lending libraries for toys and books are sometimes a feature of work with younger pupils. Many schools make positive use of parents' particular expertise to enrich pupils' learning, for example, by working with a group on a task or project, or helping to run an extra-curricular activity. Inspectors should establish the extent to which parents are involved in this way.

A check should be made on how parents are kept informed about their child's progress, including whether written reports to parents meet the statutory requirements and give clear information about pupils' attainment and progress. Opportunities for follow-up should be explored. Evidence will arise from the parents' meeting, sampling of reports and discussions with staff. The school may have examples of records of regular home-school contacts, such as reading and homework diaries and news about pupils' progress. In looking at the work of a sample of pupils it can be helpful to look at copies of reports and discuss pupils' subsequent progress with teachers.

Inspectors should establish whether parents are involved in the formal reviews of their child's progress, including transitional points in their child's educational career.

*Is the school's work enriched by links with the community?*

- Evaluation should centre on the contribution made to pupils' intellectual and personal development by the school's involvement with and contribution to the community. Links may be with a range of organisations, services and employers, through which pupils gain, for example, a greater understanding of society and the nature of citizenship. Some links may enhance particular aspects of curriculum provision by setting teaching in a work-related context.

## MAIN SOURCES OF EVIDENCE

**Before the inspection**

Evidence about parental understanding of and involvement with the work of the school can be gained through:

◆ **analysis** of the returns to the parents' questionnaire;

◆ **discussion** with parents at the pre-inspection meeting;

◆ **looking at** the prospectus, newsletters and any other information for parents, including that dealing with enquiries and complaints.

The extent of contacts with the local community may be indicated by:

◆ **the minutes of governors' meetings;**

◆ **newsletters to parents;**

◆ **teachers' planning.**

**During the inspection**

The following will provide evidence of the extent to which parents are encouraged to support their children's learning:

◆ **an examination** of annual reports to parents and arrangements for follow-up discussion;

◆ **an examination** of annual review documentation, individual education plans and care plans under the Children Act;

◆ **a scrutiny** of reading diaries or logs and other means of maintaining contact with parents over pupils' work;

◆ **discussion** with governors, staff, pupils, and parent helpers.

Contacts with the local community can be further explored through:

◆ **discussion** with staff involved in integration of pupils in mainstream schools, colleges or work experience placements;

◆ **discussion with visitors** to the school, focusing on their contribution to the curriculum and its effect on pupils' attainment and progress;

◆ **discussion with pupils** about their work, including materials in displays, relating to community projects.

**Inspection schedule**

## 6 The management and efficiency of the school

### 6.1 LEADERSHIP AND MANAGEMENT

**INSPECTORS MUST EVALUATE AND REPORT ON**

- how well the governors, headteacher, and staff with management responsibilities contribute to the quality of education provided by the school and the standards achieved by all of its pupils;

- the extent to which the school complies with statutory requirements.

*Judgements should be based on the extent to which:*

- strong leadership provides clear educational direction for the work of the school;

- teaching and curriculum development are monitored, evaluated and supported;

- the school has aims, values and policies which are reflected through all the work of the school;

- the school, through its development planning, identifies relevant priorities and targets, takes the necessary action, and monitors and evaluates its progress towards them;

- there is a positive ethos, which reflects the school's commitment to high achievement, an effective learning environment, good relationships and equality of opportunity for all pupils;

- statutory requirements are met.

## Guidance on using the schedule

### INSPECTION FOCUS

■ Evaluation should focus on the extent to which leadership and management produce an effective school: one that promotes and sustains improvement in educational standards achieved and the quality of education provided.

There are three key points about the evaluation:

◆ first, the focus is on impact rather than on intentions, although it is very important for inspectors to understand what the intentions are in order to assess how effectively they are being met;

◆ second, the judgement is about the quality and not the particular style or pattern of leadership and management in the school. Different patterns and styles of leadership and management can be equally effective;

◆ third, leadership and management should be judged as a whole, taking into account the contributions of the governing body and staff, as well as the headteacher. While the personal contribution of the headteacher is crucial, the focus of inspection should not be exclusively on what the headteacher does.

■ The way in which the roles of the governing body, headteacher and staff (including all support staff) are carried out may vary significantly in relation to school size and other factors. Definitions of the roles of governors, the headteacher and teaching staff are set out in education law; the issue for inspectors is how these roles are interpreted in the context of the particular school.

**The governing body** has specific statutory responsibilities. These are highlighted in each section of this guidance. In essence, the governing body has three main tasks: to provide a strategic view of where the school is heading; to act as a critical friend to the school; and to hold the school to account for the educational standards it achieves and the quality of education it provides.

**The headteacher** is the professional leader of the school, responsible for the direction of its work and for its day-to-day management and organisation. In an effective school the headteacher has a direct concern for the sustained improvement of quality and standards, for equality of opportunity for all pupils and for the development of policies and use of resources to achieve these ends. It is important to bear in mind that in some special schools some headteachers may work as class teachers for some of the teaching week. Opportunities for the headteacher to work with staff during the school day can be very limited and many management tasks have to be carried out when the school is not in session. The headteacher of a special school may manage a PRU and/or a wider service; the school may have several sites.

**Other staff** have leadership and management functions. Most teachers, nursery assistants and some administrative staff hold responsibility for aspects of the school's curriculum and organisation and some hold more than one, without necessarily having specialist expertise. In a well-managed school, responsibilities are clearly defined and there is effective delegation. Staff, including support staff, understand the role they are encouraged to play in the development and running of the school. In residential schools the head of care will liaise with teaching staff.

## Guidance on using the schedule

■ Overall judgements need to be based on a wide range of evidence. They must put the emphasis on the impact of leadership and management on the work of the school, particularly in relation to its core purposes of teaching and learning. Inspectors should consider leadership and management both as a whole and in terms of the co-ordination roles undertaken by staff. Inspectors should come to a clear view about the contribution which leadership and management make to the school's achievements, supported by evidence of, for example, whether the school:

- ◆ has a sense of purpose evident in all its work and the involvement of all its staff;

- ◆ appreciates its strengths and how to sustain them;

- ◆ knows its weaknesses, at school and classroom level, and how to overcome them;

- ◆ establishes its priorities and sets targets for improvement, pursues it goals and reviews its progress;

- ◆ insists that all pupils do their best and are able to play a full part in the life of the school.

In reporting the school's compliance with statutory requirements, inspectors should focus on those which are required of the appropriate authority, especially governors. Significant matters need to be included in the **key issues for action** section of the report.

## USING THE CRITERIA

*Does strong leadership provide clear educational direction for the work of the school?*

■ This criterion is not about an educational vision in the abstract but about a sense of purpose demonstrated in the work of the school.

Inspectors need to establish whether the governing body has developed a strategic view of the school's development and the extent to which the headteacher (and senior management team where applicable) provides positive leadership which gives a firm steer to the school's work. The same perspective should apply to the way co-ordinators and other managers carry out their responsibilities. Leadership is concerned with building and co-ordinating a team whose members have a common purpose, a willingness to contribute individual strengths to the common purpose and a capacity to reflect critically on what they are doing and how it can be improved.

Inspectors need evidence, first, of the extent to which governors' contributions in support of the headteacher and senior staff are informed by an understanding of their roles and of the school; and, second, of whether the proceedings of the governing body enable it to fulfil its responsibilities for strategic planning and the quality of education. Governing body papers and discussions with governors and the headteacher may illustrate particular decisions and the background to them. Identification of examples before the inspection may allow for the impact of decisions to be traced through the school's work.

**Guidance on using the schedule**

Evaluation of the role of the headteacher needs to focus on the extent to which his or her professional leadership and management are effective in those aspects of the school's work which bear most directly on the improvement of the quality of provision and the educational standards achieved. Inspectors should look for evidence of the headteacher's commitment and contribution to these areas through, for example, the management of staff and pupils, the monitoring and evaluation of classroom work and through links with parents.

Evaluation of the contribution made by staff with leadership and management roles , including the head of care in residential schools, can start with whether job descriptions are clear and realistic and the extent to which staff understand and are committed to them. Evaluation should also cover whether staff manage their responsibilities effectively in relation to the time and opportunities made available. A useful line of enquiry is the link between job descriptions, staff appraisal, staff development and the school's decision-making structure. The focus should be on what the staff with management responsibilities do to establish and improve standards and quality.

### Are teaching and curriculum development monitored, evaluated and supported?

■ This criterion applies to all staff with management responsibility. It emphasises that a test of effective leadership and management is the commitment to monitoring and evaluating teaching and the curriculum and to taking action to sustain and improve their quality.

Inspectors should assess how well this commitment is seen through at all levels. Headteachers have an important role as the leading professional and inspectors should gauge whether the headteacher is involved in the classroom and knows what goes on there. They should establish what the headteacher and other staff do to find out about the quality of provision and what they do to support and encourage colleagues, to build on good work and remedy weaknesses. Evaluating teaching and the curriculum should lead to specific intervention, for example through a change in curriculum organisation, through curriculum development, staff training, the provision of resources or intensive support for individual teachers. In some cases the action taken will necessarily be indirect.

The team needs to collect evidence through subject inspection about the effect of what is done to improve provision. The evidence will be pupils' attainment, progress and response. Examples of specific action may be drawn from:

◆ the school development plan and subject elements of it;

◆ the steps taken through the appraisal process and the staff development programme (covered in Section 6.2) to improve teaching;

◆ the outcomes of the monitoring of pupils' work and experience in school.

### Does the school have aims, values and policies which are reflected through all its work?

■ The analysis starts with whether the school has agreed and published aims which express high expectations of what pupils can achieve.

## Guidance on using the schedule

The central question is the extent to which aims, values and policies influence the work of all staff and form the basis of a shared sense of purpose. Inspectors should establish, first, how staff are involved in the formulation of aims, values and policies and of the procedures which arise from them; and, second, what steps are taken to ensure that teaching and other staff (including staff new to the school) understand them. The test is whether they are reflected in the work of the school and kept under review.

Parents' support for the school's aims and values is reflected in the parents' questionnaire and meeting. The school may have carried out surveys of the views of parents for itself, the outcomes of which may provide valuable background information.

Inspectors should also seek evidence of the extent to which pupils feel at home in the school community.

*Does the school, through its development planning, identify appropriate priorities and targets, take the necessary action and monitor and evaluate its progress towards them?*

■ Evaluation should start with the school's planning, whether in the form of a written school development plan or otherwise. There are three elements on which evaluation needs to focus:

◆ whether the school's priorities and any specific targets associated with them are appropriate – that is, whether they are the right issues to be pursuing in relation to the school's circumstances and needs;

◆ whether the school has been able to devise clear programmes of action and target resources, particularly staff time and funding for curriculum and staff development, to manage the implementation within the time intended;

◆ whether the school has sound procedures for monitoring and evaluating the outcomes of its work, including the use of quantitative data where appropriate, in order to judge the extent to which priorities are achieved.

School development planning is likely to be a useful process if it involves all staff productively in these elements of planning, implementation and review. Inspectors should decide whether, taken together, they form the basis of an effective strategy for improvement.

*Is there a positive ethos which reflects the school's commitment to high achievement, an effective learning environment, good relationships and equality of opportunity for all pupils?*

■ Inspectors should make a summary judgement about the ethos of the school, drawing on conclusions reached in relation to other sections of the Schedule, notably Section 4.2. The focus is the contribution of leadership and management to attitudes, relationships and the provision of equal opportunities. (Notes on the management of equal opportunities are given at the end of this section.)

*Are statutory requirements met?*

■ Reference should be made to the extent to which the governing body fulfils its statutory obligations.

**Guidance on using the schedule**

## MAIN SOURCES OF EVIDENCE

**Before the inspection**

◆ the *Headteacher's Form and Statement*, school prospectus and school development plan should indicate the main aims, policies and priorities of the school;

◆ **a staff handbook** (if available) may outline some of the main policies and procedures associated with the management of the school;

◆ **job descriptions (if available)** will give an initial picture of how responsibilities are expected to be carried out;

◆ **minutes of the governing body meetings** will help in forming a preliminary view of the governors' involvement in the strategic management of the school;

◆ **pre-inspection discussions** with headteachers, governors and parents should give an indication of how well the school's aims and priorities are understood and supported.

**During the inspection**

Evidence of the extent to which aims, policies and priorities are reflected in the work of the school may be gained from:

◆ **observation of lessons and the daily routines** of the school to establish the impact of management on standards and quality, and the effectiveness of equal opportunities policies;

◆ **discussions with teaching staff,** including those with senior management roles and responsibilities, subject and year group co-ordinators, to explore their role in monitoring, evaluating and intervening in the subject or aspect of work for which they have responsibility;

◆ **discussions with support staff** to gain their perceptions of, and support for, the aims and values of the school;

◆ **discussions with pupils** to gain their sense of the values of the school community.

**Guidance on using the schedule**

**ADDITIONAL NOTES**

### EQUAL OPPORTUNITIES

References to equal opportunities are made throughout the schedule and guidance. This section focuses upon the effectiveness of the school's leadership and management in overseeing the creation and implementation of policies to promote equality of opportunity and high achievements for all pupils.

Inspectors will need to evaluate:

◆ how far the school complies with relevant legislation, including the Education Act (1944), the Sex Discrimination Act (1975), the Race Relations Act (1976), the Education Act (1981), the Education Act (1986), the Children Act (1989), the Education Reform Act (1988) and subsequent case law;

◆ how well the leadership and management promote equal access by all pupils to the full range of opportunities for achievement that the school provides.

**During the inspection** the team should consider how well the school:

◆ reflects equality of opportunity in its aims and objectives, curriculum and organisation, including the grouping of pupils;

◆ monitors pupils' achievements by gender, attainment, background and ethnicity to ensure fairness of treatment;

◆ offers relevant role models to all pupils in its distribution of teachers and others within its staffing and management structures, including the allocation of curricular and other responsibilities;

◆ provides appropriate support for pupils for whom English is an additional language in order to give them access to the whole curriculum.

Evidence will need to include a scrutiny of the school's policies, staffing structures, curricular plans and pupils' records; discussions with the headteacher, other staff and pupils; direct observation of actions and relationships in and out of classrooms; consideration of the educational standards achieved by pupils, including examination and other test results; and consideration of the quality of provision under other sections of the schedule.

### SPECIAL EDUCATIONAL NEEDS

Inspectors will need to check that the school has regard to the *1994 Code of Practice on the identification and assessment of special educational need* and to the earlier relevant sections of the 1993, 1988 and 1981 Education Acts. Discussions with the headteacher and governors, together with a scrutiny of the school's policies and plans, will show whether the school complies with the following requirements:

◆   that in co-operation with the headteacher, the governing body must determine the school's policy and approach for special educational needs, set up appropriate staffing and funding arrangements and maintain general oversight of the provision;

◆   that the governing body's annual report informs parents about the success of the special educational needs policy and any significant changes to it; any consultation with the LEA, funding authority or other schools; and the allocation of resources over the previous year to pupils with special educational needs.

**Inspection schedule**

## 6.2 STAFFING, ACCOMMODATION AND LEARNING RESOURCES

### INSPECTORS MUST EVALUATE AND REPORT ON

■ the adequacy of staffing, accommodation and learning resources, highlighting strengths and weaknesses in different subjects and areas of the curriculum, where they affect the quality of education provided and the educational standards achieved.

*Judgements should be based on the extent to which:*

◆ the number, qualifications and experience of teachers and other classroom staff match the demands of the curriculum;

◆ arrangements for the induction, appraisal and professional development of staff contribute to their effectiveness;

◆ the accommodation allows the curriculum to be taught effectively;

◆ learning resources are adequate for the school's curriculum and range of pupils.

## Guidance on using the schedule

### INSPECTION FOCUS

■ The report needs to evaluate the extent to which the school is staffed and resourced to teach the curriculum effectively, and whether there are any clear features which contribute to or detract from quality and standards. Judgements on the effective use of staff, accommodation and learning resources should be included in Section 6.3.

■ **Staffing** accounts for a high proportion of the school budget. The work of teachers is supported by classroom assistants and other staff. Although the two groups have distinct roles, their work is complementary. Effective team-working means each member has a clear understanding of their own roles and responsibilities and those of others.

In residential schools there must be a qualified head of care. Sufficient and suitable night-time supervision should be provided; this may include a waking member of staff.

The provision of multidisciplinary support and medical input should reflect the requirements of pupils' needs. Additional support may be provided for pupils for whom English is an additional language.

There are no statutory standards for assessing the adequacy of **teaching accommodation.** DFEE bulletins give advice on space and other features. The accommodation must conform with building regulations, meet health and safety regulations and allow the school to provide the statutory curriculum. The Education (School Premises) Regulations 1981 apply to all schools catering for pupils with special educational need. For independent schools catering mainly or wholly for pupils with SEN, reference must be made to the Education (Special Educational Need) (Approval of Independent Schools) Regulations 1994 and guidance contained in DFE Circular 3/94.

Most pupils in nursery and primary years spend the greater part of the day in one classroom base; this may be open-plan or shared with another class. The size of the classroom has an impact on the quality of the learning environment, as do the equipment, facilities and services provided. The adequacy of indoor and outdoor provision for play and PE vary considerably from school to school.

**Learning resources** should be appropriate in range, quality and quantity and deployed well. Some pupils' statements of special educational need may identify specific additional items of equipment and teaching support. Adaptations may have to be made to accommodation and furniture to meet the needs of pupils with physical or sensory disabilities.

■ Overall judgements should identify the strengths of the school's staffing, accommodation and learning resources and highlight shortfalls which affect the standards achieved and the quality of education provided. The report should only describe aspects of a school's provision for this purpose.

## Guidance on using the schedule

## USING THE CRITERIA

*Do the number, qualifications and experience of teachers and other classroom staff match the demands of the curriculum?*

■ The staff as a whole should have sufficient knowledge and expertise to meet the requirements of the school's curriculum, including areas of learning for the under-fives, the National Curriculum across all key stages, religious education and post-16 courses. Staff also need knowledge and expertise to cover other aspects of the school curriculum, such as personal, social, health and careers education. Inspectors should take into account the extent to which the school maximises available subject and phase expertise to cover the school curriculum and knowledge of particular disabilities.

Inspectors should assess the extent to which the level of staffing enables the curriculum to be taught effectively to all pupils in appropriately-sized teaching groups for the specific disability, as described in DES Circular 11/90.

They should also consider whether there are enough appropriately skilled support and care staff to enable teaching, administration and the day-to-day life of the school to function effectively, and the extent to which curriculum support staff and residential care officers work with teachers in planning, teaching and recording pupils' progress.

Inspectors should investigate whether staff are suitably qualified and experienced and, in the case of hearing and visual impairment, hold relevant specialist qualifications which meet statutory requirements. Inspectors should establish whether teaching staff who work with pupils for whom English is an additional language are experienced and qualified for such work. Judgements need to be made about the effectiveness of staff deployment and whether there is sufficient non-contact time for planning, reviewing and undertaking co-ordinating functions. Judgements need to be made about the appropriateness and quality of additional staffing resources, such as therapy or medical support, where provided in response to individual statements of special educational need.

*Do arrangements for the induction, appraisal and professional development of staff contribute to their effectiveness?*

■ In all schools, but particularly where there is a high staff turnover, inspectors should enquire into the adequacy of the arrangements for inducting all staff new to the school, and for those assuming new roles and responsibilities. In the case of newly qualified teachers, inspectors should establish whether the induction arrangements take account of DFEE guidance.

Procedures for teacher appraisal should be in line with requirements. Appraisal (including the appraisal of support staff where a scheme is in place) should help staff evaluate and improve their practice. Inspectors do not have access to individual appraisal records. Inspectors should look for evidence of the contribution of professional development to the quality of teaching.

Attention should also be given to the effectiveness of the staff development and in-service training programme in motivating staff and in identifying and meeting individual and corporate needs.

*Does the accommodation including specialist accommodation and facilities for outdoor activities allow the curriculum to be taught effectively?*

■ Accommodation should be inspected in terms of its adequacy for the numbers on roll and ages of pupils as well as the range of curriculum activities. Judgements about accommodation should be made against the recognised accommodation (RA) set for the school by the DFEE. Account should be taken of the regulations set out in the Education (School Premises) Regulations 1981 SFI 909, the guidance provided in Building Bulletin 77 (BB 77) and the Approval Schedules used for the inspection of independent schools who wish to be approved under Section 189 (1) The Education Act 1993. Coverage should include the arrangements made to use specialist accommodation off-site.

Inspectors must ensure that class bases and specialist areas are accessible for all disabilities; that provision of day and evening toilet facilities are in accordance with regulations; that changing facilities for those pupils with profound disabilities have suitable privacy; and the quality of residential provision is fit for purpose.

The team should come to a view about the quality of accommodation, including outdoor areas, and whether it provides a stimulating and well-maintained learning environment. Particular attention should be given to how well the accommodation, furniture and acoustics enable pupils with physical and sensory disabilities to access all areas of the curriculum.

*Are learning resources adequate for the school's curriculum and range of pupils?*

■ Inspectors should judge whether the level of provision, deployment and condition of books, materials and equipment held centrally and in classrooms enhances or detracts from the quality of the work in different subjects or areas of learning, and if the range of resources is appropriate to pupils' age and needs. Good-quality resources will reflect the interests of pupils and present gender and cultural diversity in a positive way; they should be readily accessible to staff and pupils.

The team should judge whether the library or learning resource centre is adequately resourced to enable it to play a central role in supporting learning. (Notes on school libraries are given at the end of this section.)

The provision of information technology resources across the curriculum and their use to support learning should also be assessed by the whole team. In some schools, pupils will be provided with technological communication aids; their adequacy should be checked.

For vocational courses at KS4 and post-16, inspectors should consider the extent to which students have access to learning resources to support the independent learning requirements of their courses.

In residential schools, inspectors will need to judge whether the level of resourcing provides adequately for pupils' leisure and extra-curricular experiences.

Most schools use resources beyond the school, including museums, galleries and field centres, to enrich the curriculum. Judgements about the effectiveness of their use will usually be based on discussion and scrutiny of work.

## Guidance on using the schedule

## MAIN SOURCES OF EVIDENCE

### Before the inspection

◆ the *Headteacher's Form and Statement* gives the number, qualifications and experience of teachers and details of support staff and care staff where relevant;

◆ a sample of staff **job descriptions**;

◆ a **staff handbook** or staff development plan (if available) may give useful information about the induction, appraisal and professional development of staff;

◆ the **preliminary visit** will give initial impressions of staffing, accommodation and learning resources and may raise some views to be followed up later;

◆ **pre-inspection meetings** with governors, headteacher and parents are likely to raise issues about staffing, accommodation and resources.

### During the inspection

Further evidence should be gathered through:

◆ **observation of lessons** to evaluate the effects of any arrangements/exchanges of teachers to provide specialist teaching, and the quality of liaison between teachers, and between teachers and support staff;

◆ **a scrutiny of timetables** to collect information on the deployment of teachers, classroom assistants and visiting specialists;

◆ **discussion with teachers** and support staff about any arrangements for continuing professional development;

◆ **an examination of planning documents** to assess the impact of joint planning arrangements on the quality of planning;

◆ **a survey** of all the available accommodation and facilities on the school site including classrooms, corridors, work areas, halls, sensory, soft play and other specialist rooms, playing fields, environmental areas and playgrounds, and any additional adaption for pupils with specific needs. Consideration should be given as to whether the provision enhances or constrains the quality of education provided. An evaluation should be made of the impact of any decisions taken by the school about its accommodation;

◆ **a scrutiny** of school/class libraries, reading materials, textbooks, resource collections, outdoor play equipment, museum/art loans, natural and historical artefacts to assess their impact on the breadth of the curriculum and its ability to address the needs of all pupils.

**ADDITIONAL NOTES**

## SCHOOL LIBRARIES

Many special schools have a central library holding fiction and non-fiction books and often audio, video and computer materials as well. A number of schools use loans , often of special interest collections, from a schools' library service. Some schools, particularly small ones, may not have the accommodation to provide a central library. Most nursery and primary classrooms should have book areas, with collections of fiction, non-fiction books and other texts. The quality and use of both types of provision need to be inspected, but with a focus on how the provision affects the children's attainment as well as teaching and learning.

Inspectors need to sample the range of the library stock to form a view of whether there are enough books to support the curriculum and if they are suitable for the age range of pupils and their competence as readers. They need to decide if the materials are likely to stimulate the interest and intellectual development of the pupils. The *Headteacher's Form* includes the ratio of books to pupils and this will give a clue about the adequacy of provision, but more important is the investigation of the use of both the library and classroom provision, and their match to the children's needs.

Inspectors should see pupils using the library provision in a range of contexts. They should check that the library stocks are accessible when the children need to use them. They need to watch how confidently pupils find what they need and how they select books and other resources. Inspectors need to determine how the organisation of the library helps pupils to make the most effective use of it, and whether library use is taught and encouraged in lessons.

**Inspection schedule**

## 6.3 THE EFFICIENCY OF THE SCHOOL

**INSPECTORS MUST EVALUATE AND REPORT ON**

- the efficiency and effectiveness with which the resources made available to the school are managed, including the use made of specific grants, and the allocation and use of funds for its pupils[28].

- the extent to which the school provides value for money.

*Judgements should be based on the extent to which:*

- educational developments are supported through careful financial planning;

- effective use is made of staff, accommodation and learning resources;

- there is efficient financial control and school administration;

- the school provides value for money in terms of the educational standards achieved and quality of education provided in relation to its context and income.

---

28  Where a school's budget is in deficit or has an undue surplus, the report should record this together with the school's reasons and, where appropriate, the measures being taken to address this matter.

## Guidance on using the schedule

### INSPECTION FOCUS

- An efficient school makes good use of all its available resources to achieve the best possible educational outcomes for all its pupils – and in doing so provides excellent value for money. This section calls for a summative judgement on the basis of the findings on all aspects of the school's work.

- Locally-managed LEA-maintained or grant-maintained special schools have considerable discretion over their spending. Their governing bodies have direct responsibility for oversight of financial management: their task is to ensure that the school can account for the expenditure to which it is committed, that it budgets systematically for new expenditure and that it regularly analyses the use of resources. Where appropriate, inspectors should be conversant with the differences in financial regulations and responsibilities between LEA and GM schools.

  The sources of funding and patterns of expenditure in LEA-maintained special schools may be complicated by the devolution (sometimes outside formal delegation) of funding for services which form discretionary elements of the Potential Schools Budget (the PSB). For all schools there may also be grant funding from GEST and some funding from other sources, such as the Single Regeneration Budget, City Challenge, European Union and Section 11 schemes.

  Each special school, including those in the independent sector approved under Section 186(1) of the Education Act 1993, will have a budget set either through the LEA Local Management of Schools formula, the Funding Authority for Schools, or as a result of the fees levied for individual pupils.

  The post-16 pattern may include joint provision with other schools and/or with FEFC sector colleges. Consortium, franchising or purchasing arrangements may be the most cost-effective ways of providing vocational or other courses.

  Unit costs expressed in the LMSS schemes for any one disability group will vary between LEAs, as will fees in independent and non-maintained schools. Comparisons, therefore, between schools serving similar disabilities are complex, difficult to validate and are, therefore, **inappropriate.**

- Overall judgements need to recognise that schools face financial constraints and choices. The key task is to assess the impact of the school's decisions: the way the available funding is used in relation to its educational priorities and to effect improvement. Judgements should cover the deployment of staff and the use of accommodation and learning resources. Attention should be given to the use of specific grants.

  Close consideration should be given to budget planning where the school has a significant surplus or a significant deficit on its current budget. The report should record the reasons given by the school for this position, and the action it is intending to take. In analysing any surplus, inspectors should take account of committed expenditure which may not yet have been invoiced and of the school's budgeting for major expenditure in the future. Although prudent management requires contingency funding, a surplus exceeding 5% of income should be carefully evaluated. Any significant deficit needs to be viewed in the light of the school's likely budget prospects and, in the case of LEA-maintained schools, the LEA's policy on planned overspend.

  Value for money can only be judged after considering all the inspection evidence about the educational standards achieved and the quality of education provided, and setting this in relation to the school's context and income. In independent schools, inspectors should judge whether the total income arising from all fees is used to give value for money.

**Guidance on using the schedule**

## USING THE CRITERIA

*Are educational developments supported through careful financial planning?*

■ Evaluation against this criterion needs to be seen in relation to Sections 6.1 and 6.2.

Inspectors should review the funding available to the school in the previous and current year through the delegated local management formula budget share or the annual maintenance grant, together with any further devolved funding, specific grants or other income.

Inspectors should examine the use of the funding for different purposes, including provision for teaching staff, support staff, curriculum development, learning resources and premises.

An effective process of school development planning will focus on improving educational outcomes and relate expenditure to this. Even where the room for manoeuvre on the use of funding is marginal, the school should be able to demonstrate that it budgets systematically for new and well-focused expenditure, for example on learning resources, rather than relying on previous patterns – but minute detail should not be expected. Inspectors should look for evidence of the school planning ahead. Depending on when the inspection falls it would be reasonable to expect detailed planning to be under way for the forthcoming year, with outline planning for at least one or two years beyond.

Inspectors should consider how the governing body is fulfilling its strategic responsibility for planning the use of resources. The key to the judgement will be whether financial planning is based on good current data and sound projections, whether consideration has been given to alternative strategies for managing expenditure and for handling contingencies, and whether the school is clear about priorities. Inspectors should also assess the extent to which staff with management responsibility are involved in or informed about financial planning.

*Is effective use made of staff, accommodation and learning resources?*

■ Inspectors need to draw on the inspection of the other aspects of the school, especially the evidence from subject inspection, to determine how well the resources of staff (including care staff where relevant), accommodation and learning resources are used. Both provision and use can be a guide to the quality of planning in the past.

Particular attention should be given to:

◆ the efficiency of the school's staffing arrangements, taking into account curriculum organisation, grouping arrangements and contact time;

◆ the deployment of additional teaching staff for pupils for whom English is an additional language, including any staff financed through specific grants.

*Is there efficient financial control and school administration?*

■ Detailed advice on financial administration is given in *Keeping Your Balance: Standards for Financial Administration in Schools*. Schools are asked to complete the financial questionnaire which forms part of the *Headteacher's Statement*.

Inspectors should establish whether the main recommendations in the latest audit report available to the school have been acted on. They are not expected to undertake a detailed check on the school's financial procedures themselves and should not become preoccupied with them. The judgement should focus on whether financial administration is sound and uses a minimum of management time so that adequate information is available to the headteacher and governors and finances are kept in good order.

Schools are increasingly likely to have computerised financial management systems which allow for modelling of expenditure projections and provide sophisticated accounting. Not all schools have or need such systems with which to control a budget with a high level of committed expenditure and limited flexibility.

Inspectors should evaluate the school's administrative procedures. At best, they should be unobtrusive, resulting in efficient day-to-day organisation and the capacity to respond to the unforeseen event. Administration is at its best where it gives clear support to the central purposes of the school, keeping the way clear for teachers to focus on their work with pupils and supporting their endeavours.

### *Does the school provide value for money in terms of educational standards achieved and quality of education provided in relation to the its context and income?*

■ The value for money afforded by the school is a summative judgement which relates the educational standards achieved to the pupils' capabilities, and the quality of education provided by a school to its income, taking account of any appropriate contextual factors.

Judgements should be based on the team's conclusions about:

◆ pupils' attainment and progress, attitudes to learning, behaviour, personal development and attendance;

◆ the quality of education provided and the effectiveness with which staffing, accommodation and learning resources are used;

◆ the cost-effectiveness of major spending decisions.

The table on page 124 may be useful in ordering judgements.

## Guidance on using the schedule

### EVALUATING VALUE FOR MONEY

The table uses key judgement recording statements. A school giving the very best value for money would have judgements on contextual factors coded as 7 and judgements on outcomes, provision and expenditure coded as 1, and average unit costs.

| Judgement recording grade | | 1 | 2 | 3 | 4 | 5 | 6 | 7 | |
|---|---|---|---|---|---|---|---|---|---|
| **CONTEXTUAL FACTORS** | | | | | | | | | |
| The socio-economic circumstances of pupils are: | Very favourable | * | * | * | * | * | * | * | Very unfavourable |
| The attainment of the intake on entry is: | Very high | * | * | * | * | * | * | * | Very low |
| **OUTCOMES** | | | | | | | | | |
| Pupils' progress is: | Excellent | * | * | * | * | * | * | * | Very poor |
| The attitudes, behaviour and personal development of pupils at the school are: | Excellent | * | * | * | * | * | * | * | Very poor |
| **PROVISION** | | | | | | | | | |
| The quality of education particularly teaching, provided by the school is: | Excellent | * | * | * | * | * | * | * | Very poor |
| **EXPENDITURE** | | | | | | | | | |
| Unit cost for a school of this type and size is: | Very low | * | * | * | * | * | * | * | Very high |
| **VALUE FOR MONEY JUDGEMENT** | | | | | | | | | |
| The value for money provided by the school is: | Excellent | * | * | * | * | * | * | * | Very poor |

**Guidance on using the schedule**

## MAIN SOURCES OF EVIDENCE

### Before the inspection

◆ the *Headteacher's Form* and *Statement* will provide the context for forming preliminary views on efficiency;

◆ **school documentation** on financial planning and administration, budgetary information, including out-turn statements, and copies of auditors' reports will all provide important background information;

◆ **the school development plan** should indicate whether the school has set clear objectives for the main tasks it faces, has identified the resources needed to achieve them, and has evaluated its work, spending and cost-effectiveness;

◆ **minutes of governing body meetings** may help to determine the governors' role in maintaining the efficiency of the school;

◆ **pre-inspection meetings** with governors, the headteacher and parents provide opportunities to explore some of the issues emerging from a reading of the documentation.

### During the inspection

◆ **further discussions** with governors, headteacher and other staff should help to determine how major budgetary, staffing or resource decisions were taken, how they were implemented and with what effect;

◆ **general observations** of lessons and school routines will provide evidence of the impact on the quality of education of decisions made about the provision and use of resources;

◆ **scrutiny** of equipment inventories.

**Inspection schedule**

# PART B: CURRICULUM AREAS AND SUBJECTS

## 7 Areas of learning for children under five

### FOR PUPILS UNDER FIVE, THE REPORT MUST INCLUDE EVALUATION OF

- the strengths and weaknesses in attainment, pupils' attitudes, teaching and other provision across the areas of learning.

## 8 English, mathematics and science

### FOR EACH SUBJECT THE REPORT MUST INCLUDE EVALUATION OF

- pupils' attainment, drawing on evidence of what pupils know, understand and can do by the end of the relevant stage;

- progress made in relation to pupils' prior attainment;

- pupils' attitudes to learning;

- any strengths and weaknesses in teaching and other factors which contribute to the standards achieved in the subject.

In English, the subject report should also draw on evidence of the contribution made by other subjects to pupils' competence in reading, writing, speaking and listening. In mathematics, the report should draw on evidence of the use of number in other subjects.

## 9 Other Subjects

### FOR EACH SUBJECT OR COURSE INSPECTED, THE REPORT MUST INCLUDE EVALUATION OF

- each of the aspects indicated above where there is sufficient evidence.

In this section, subjects may be grouped or reported on separately, as is appropriate to the size of the school, the way it organises teaching, and the extent of the evidence available.

In information technology, the report should draw on evidence from all the other subjects inspected.

**Guidance on using the schedule**

## INSPECTION FOCUS

■ The inspection of subjects and courses of the curriculum and the provision for pupils under five should focus on pupils' attainment and progress; teaching and other aspects of provision which make a significant contribution to what is achieved; and pupils' response.

■ **For pupils under five** inspection should include the provision made for them and their attainment and progress in relation to the areas of learning. They are:

- linguistic and literary;
- mathematical;
- scientific and technological;
- creative and aesthetic;
- physical;
- human and social;
- moral and spiritual.

National Curriculum subjects, together with RE[29] and any provision specified in the inspection contract, must be inspected.

**For the primary age range,** the organisation of the curriculum varies from school to school. Often, subjects are embedded within themes or topics. It is important that, whatever the form of organisation, the attainment and progress and the quality of provision, particularly teaching, in subjects of the National Curriculum are evaluated. With the exception of English, mathematics and science, however, registered inspectors may choose to group subjects together for reporting purposes. If this is done, the evaluation of the separate subjects must be clear.

Inspection of National Curriculum subjects must be based on knowledge and understanding by inspectors of the National Curriculum subject Orders. Inspection of non-denominational RE will be in relation to the relevant agreed syllabus, and inspectors need to have knowledge of this.

**For the secondary age range,** the organisation of the curriculum is mainly subject-based although there may in addition be personal and social education courses and vocational courses at KS4. It is important that, whatever the form of organisation, the attainment and progress and the quality of provision, particularly teaching, in subjects of the National Curriculum are evaluated and reported upon.

A separate report should be written on each subject or course in all but exceptional circumstances. In the cases where subjects are grouped, a clear evaluation of each subject must be included.

---

[29]   The 1992 Act as amended by Section 259 of the 1993 Act makes separate provision for the inspection of denominational religious education in those schools where it is provided; such inspection falls under Section 13 of the 1992 Act.

## Guidance on using the schedule

Inspection of National Curriculum subjects must be based on knowledge and understanding by inspectors of the National Curriculum subject Orders. Inspection of non-denominational RE will be in relation to the relevant agreed syllabus, and inspectors need to have knowledge of this. Inspectors also need to be familiar with the requirements of GCSE and other relevant qualifications.

**Post-16** provision may include A/AS-level, GNVQ or NVQ courses, as well as GCSE and other courses. Inspection must be based on knowledge and understanding by inspectors of the nature and requirements of these courses.

*In relation to the inspection schedule, inspectors should concentrate in particular on the following aspects:*

### 4.1 Attainment and progress

The focus should be on attainment and progress in each subject or area of learning for pupils under five and in each key stage. The criteria appropriate to the age range should form the basis for judgments, and reporting should include comment on any unusual variations in attainment and progress for different groups of pupils.

### 4.2 Pupils' attitudes to learning, their behaviour and personal development

All the criteria should be applied. Judgements will be made in each lesson or session and in relation to the subject as a whole.

### 5.1 Teaching

This is a key aspect of provision on which a judgement in each subject or area of learning or at each key stage is needed. All the criteria should be applied, and overall judgements for the subject drawn from observations in individual lessons or sessions.

*The subject report should only include reference to other aspects of the schedule if there are particular strengths or weaknesses.*

*Inspectors must be fully conversant with the National Curriculum requirements for the subjects they inspect, and the contents of any guidance issued by OFSTED or the School Curriculum and Assessment Authority on the inspection, teaching or assessment of those subjects.*

**Inspection schedule**

# PART C: INSPECTION DATA

## 10 Summary of inspection evidence

### THE REPORT MUST INCLUDE

a concise, factual statement summarising the number of inspectors; the number of inspector days spent gathering first-hand evidence; the total time spent in classes, discussion with pupils and evaluation of their work; and a brief comment about other evidence.

It may be appropriate to refer to the timing of the inspection and any interruption in the normal programme of the school. Where a subject or area of learning is not being taught at the time of the inspection, or where other exceptional circumstances reduce the coverage of inspection, the report should state this clearly.

## 11 Data and indicators

### THE REPORT MUST INCLUDE

PUPILS

Number of pupils on roll

Number of pupils having a statement of special educational need

Number of pupils on the special educational needs register (except special schools)

Number of full-time pupils eligible for free school meals

TEACHERS AND CLASSES

Number of qualified teachers (full-time equivalent)

Number of pupils per qualified teacher

Number of classroom support staff (primary, special and nursery schools)

Average class size (primary and nursery schools)

FINANCIAL DATA

Summary balance sheet, including expenditure per pupil, for the latest available financial year. Not required for schools which do not have a fully delegated budget.

PARENTAL SURVEY

A summary of the responses to the parents' questionnaire (when issued)

## Guidance on using the schedule

## PARENTS' QUESTIONNAIRE

Registered inspectors are now required to report the results of the parents questionnaire, when it has been used, in section 11 of the report of the inspection. It will also be included in the summary of the report.

**All reporting of the questionnaires must include the number of questionnaires sent out, the number returned and the percentage return rate.**

In most cases the report should include a table setting out, for each question, the percentage of ticks in each column. There should also be a short commentary on any other issues raised by parents on the forms.

Registered inspectors must exercise particular care in reporting the results of the questionnaire when numbers of returns are small. Small numbers of returns are unlikely to be statistically significant and should not be used as the basis for generalisations. There is also a potential problem with the confidentiality of the responses. In a very small school, or where the response has been small, it may be possible to identify individual responses from a detailed breakdown.

**Where there are small numbers of returned questionnaires, a short verbal summary of the responses will suffice.**

It is difficult to be precise about the numbers involved, and registered inspectors will need to use their judgement about the circumstances of each school, but usually **a minimum of 20 returned questionnaires** are needed.

# INDEX